LIFE IN THE UNITED STATE
FROM CHILDHOOD TO MA

1945   1946

1947   1948

LIFE IN THE UNITED STATES NAVY
FROM CHILDHOOD TO MANHOOD

CHAPTER I

LIFE OF THE CHILD

Jack L. McSherry, Jr., born in Shamokin, Pennsylvania in the year 1928, son of Ivy and Jack McSherry, lived during the entire time of the great depression in a house which they purchased in a small village near Shamokin, called Sunnyside.

Even though the country was in a turmoil because of the Depression, Jack was a happy child living in Sunnyside. He attended grammar school in a country school in the nearby village of Overlook. All the students in that school were country people. Everyone in the school knew everyone else. There were four dedicated teachers for the eight grades, but with proper organization, this system of teaching worked. All of Jack's closest friends also attended that school. They were together all day in school. After school, and in the evenings and weekends, they were also together.

Being a country school, unlike the city schools, they attended school from September to May, a period of eight months. The reason for this was so they would be available in early spring to help on the farm. However, Jack did not live on a farm, and neither did most of his close friends, so they had four months of summertime vacation to enjoy themselves together.

With a lifestyle like that, is it no wonder that Jack was upset and dismayed at the prospect of moving from that location to another. Jack's mother had a brother, Bertlette, Jack's uncle, who was a school teacher in the nearby region called Coal Township. It is rather certain that he discussed the school system with Jack's mother because Jack's older brother, Bill, had graduated from the eighth grade and was now going to attend high school. As a result, Jack's mother made the decision to move to nearby Tharptown, which was in Coal Township so that Bill could attend the Coal Township High School which, apparently, they believed was a superior school to the Ralpho Township High School which they would have attended if they had remained in Sunnyside.

As a result, in 1939, the McSherry family moved to a house in the Village of Tharptown. The new house was built and owned by Jack's grandfather. The McSherrys rented this house. The new location was more urban than Sunnyside. The kids attending the schools were urban kids, and Jack was out of place.

So Jack and his brother, David, attended the grammar school in Tharptown, and Bill attended Coal Township High School. Jack tolerated the new school but really was not happy there. Every evening after school, he would ride his bike about two miles, or hike over the mountain to Sunnyside to be with his friends.

Eventually Jack graduated from the grammar school in Tharptown and began attending Coal Township High School. He could not compare Coal Township High School with the Ralpho Township High School because he did not attend the Ralpho Township High School. However, he never thought of the Coal Township High School as being anything superior. He made school-time friends at the new High School, but his evenings were spent with his real friends, the country kids in

Sunnyside. He always believed that he would have been much happier attending high school with his real friends, and his education would have been just as good.

So, the family lived in Tharptown. Life went on and the kids found things to do and places to go. Since their grandfather worked for the water company, the kids were allowed to wander, at their pleasure, into the totally natural lands of the water company, which were a short distance from the McSherry house. There they played in the streams, watched the animals and wandered to their delight. In the wintertime, they ice skated on the dams. Friends from Sunnyside, Overlook and Weigh Scales would come and spend time with them. Everything was beginning to become happy living again.

At this time, World War 2 had begun in Europe. The Nazi's were getting very nasty, and the bombing of England was ferocious. The United States was very sympathetic toward England and assisted them as much as possible without entering the war.

Mr. McSherry, Jack's father, first enlisted in the Navy in 1907. He went around the world with President Theodore Roosevelt's Great White Fleet. The Great White Fleet, consisting of sixteen battleships, all painted white, cruised around the world on a goodwill and show of force tour, leaving Hampton Roads, Virginia on December 14, 1907 and returned to the United States on February 22, 1909.

The Great White Fleet in the Pacific Ocean

Crewman Jack L. McSherry, on
right, Aboard the USS Minnesota
with the Great White Fleet

Mr. McSherry received this certificate for crossing the equator during the Great White Fleet's cruise around the world.

The Navy loaned Mr. McSherry to the U. S. Bureau of Fisheries in the years 2011-2012 to be a crew member of the Albatross for a scientific voyage to the waters around Alaska. The Albatross was a sailing vessel, but had coal burning engines for backup. The object of the voyage was to study sea life in the waters of Alaska.

The Albatross

In 1914, his ship at that time, the USS Milwaukee, was engaged in the action involving an American invasion into Vera Cruz, Mexico.

In 1917, he served on the USS Columbia, a protected cruiser, in the Atlantic during World War I. Later in 1917, he was detached from the Columbia and loaned to the British Navy, on board the HMS Danube, to assist with navigation during convoy operations off the US East coast. During the war, in 1918, he served aboard the USS Aeolus which was a captured German ocean liner with the name Grosser Kurfurst. He was later on board the USS Kroonland in 1918 and 1919. The Aeolus and the Kroonland were transport ships which carried troops to whatever their destination may be.

After World War I, he was transferred from the Atlantic Fleet to the Pacific Fleet. He served on board the USS Helena, a gunboat, in the waters around China during the years 1920 and 1921, including cruises up and down the Yangtse River. In 1922, he was transferred to the USS Borie. During this time period, he spent time in the Philippines and in Siberia.

He finally left the active Navy Service in 1923 and enlisted in the Fleet Reserve. In 1937, he retired from the Navy after thirty years of service.

Jack L. McSherry
World War I- 1918

Jack L. McSherry
US Navy 1922

In May 1941, Mr. McSherry had some news for his family. He told them that he received a letter in the mail from the Navy Department which ordered him to report to the Philadelphia Navy Yard for active duty. Now, seven months before the attack on Pearl Harbor and the entrance of the United States into World War II, he was again serving the country in the United States Navy. His family was very proud of him, but they certainly would have preferred that he was with them at home. Jack missed his father. Mr. McSherry served in the Navy throughout the war and was finally discharged in November 1946.

On December 7, 1941, Japan attacked Pearl Harbor. The news came on the radio. Mom was listening to the news. Jack was in the attic at the time, so Mom called to him to come downstairs, which he did. At about that time the neighbor lady, having heard the news, came over to the McSherry house. The three of them listened to the news, which was all bad. They were horrified by the news and were worried about Mr. McSherry.

In the days that followed, the war continued and all of the news was bad news, as it would be over the next six months.

Mr. McSherry was assigned to the crew of the USS Roller, and later to the USS Skimmer, both mine sweepers, and for a good portion of the war was searching for mines in the Atlantic Ocean. They periodically found mines, which they cut loose from their anchorage, and destroyed them by shooting them with their fifty caliber machine gun and exploding them.

Young men were being drafted for service in the Armed Forces. Jack's Uncle David, at the age of 33, was drafted into the Army. Almost the entire family of Ivy McSherry's sister, Beulah Fertig, were drafted or enlisted into the service. The first to go was her daughter, Eleanor, who was a registered nurse. She enlisted in the Army as a nurse and a second lieutenant. Orville was drafted into the Army, next was Calvin, who was drafted into the Army and spent the war with Merrill's Marauders in the China Burma area. Marlin was drafted in the army. He was a sharpshooter and was assigned as a sniper in Europe and was wounded in action twice during the war, but survived. Lamar enlisted in the Marines and spent the war invading the islands of the Pacific. Families throughout the country were experiencing the same thing.

Jack L. McSherry
World War II

Keep 'Em Frying!

At the home front, everyone cooperated to assist in the war effort. Gasoline was rationed. Those who did not go to work, such as Mrs. McSherry and Jack, who was still in school, received stamps to purchase three gallons of gas per week. Those who worked were allotted more gas. It was impossible to buy tires for the car. Food items, such as meat, butter, sugar and coffee were rationed, and were scarce.

Mrs. McSherry went to the local hospital where she volunteered to help, without pay. However, her experience and learning opportunities at the hospital, after working at the Hospital for several years, were the primary reason that she later became a registered practical nurse.

Jack's brother, Bill, graduated from high school in 1943, then he enlisted in the Navy. He went into the Pacific on board the USS Guam, a Battle Cruiser. The war in the Pacific at that time was ferocious. Bill was in the brutal Battle of Okinawa, but survived the war.

At home, Jack helped to gather aluminum for the war effort. Mr. Dockey had a pick-up truck which he provided to, and drove for, the kids who went from house to house and asked people to contribute old aluminum pots and other items of aluminum to help in the war effort. They were very successful every time they made the rounds. People wanted to help.

Austin Chaundy, of Sunnyside, was drafted into the Army in early 1944 and sent to Europe to be with a tank division. On the 16th of December, 1944, he was killed in France when his tank was hit and exploded.

Jack's brother, David, graduated from high school in 1944, then enlisted in the Navy. He was assigned to the crew of the USS Shamrock Bay, an aircraft carrier. The Shamrock Bay transported fighter planes, and other supplies, to the battle front in North Africa.

All during the war, periodically the local officials would conduct a blackout. When the alarm sounded, everyone had to turn out all of the lights in the house and stay inside. The only people in the streets were the volunteer air-raid wardens.

Delmar Bailey, of Sunnyside, was serving in the Navy on board a destroyer in the Battle of Okinawa, in May of 1945. His destroyer was attacked by Japanese suicide planes, known as kamakazies. Although the ship fought back against the kamakazies, and shot many of them down, over a short period of time, they were hit by three diving kamakazies and were sunk into the sea. Delmar Bailey went down with the ship.

Bad news such as this was rampant during the war. Heartbreak was common, but the United States fought on.

In 1945, Jack was a senior in high school, but was only 16 years old. In March, on his seventeenth birthday, Jack and his friend from Sunnyside, Harry Harper, and, a friend from Coal Township High School, George Miller went to Harrisburg, Pennsylvania, to enlist in the Navy. Jack drove his father's 1939 Buick to Harrisburg with his passengers, Harry Harper and George Miller. He also had his mother as a passenger because, at seventeen, he was too young to enlist in the Navy without parental permission. Jack's mother reluctantly signed for him.

In Harrisburg, they were required to take a very complete physical examination. Jack's eyes were good, but he didn't want to take any chances, so he memorized the bottom line of the eye chart. It read APEORTDZ. He passed the eye exam without any problems and without the help of his memory. George Miller followed next. Apparently he also memorized the bottom line of the chart, so when he supposedly read the bottom line of the eye chart, he wasn't even looking in the direction of the chart. He was gaping around somewhere else and babbled out the letters of the bottom line. The examiners noticed and made him redo the eye test. All three passed the physical, although George was told to gain some weight. They were sent home to await notification to report for duty.

Even though the three of them enlisted together, they were separated immediately. For basic training (boot training) Harry was sent to the Great Lakes Naval Base, Jack was sent to the Bainbridge Naval Base in Maryland, and two weeks later, George Miller was also sent to Bainbridge, but in a different Regiment than Jack.

RECRUIT IDENTIFICATION CARD
NAVPERS-682 (9-43)

23 MAR 1945

INSTRUCTIONS: Keep this card carefully and deliver it to the officer to whom you report at the training station. If you fail to do so, you and others will be seriously inconvenienced.

U. S. NAVY RECRUITING STATION
FIC, Harrisburg, Pa.   2 48 72 96

TO IDENTIFY (NAME OF RECRUIT)   RATE
MC SHERRY Jack Lawrence, Jr.   AS V6 SV U. S. N. R.

COLOR OF HAIR | COLOR OF EYES | HEIGHT | WEIGHT
              | | INCHES | POUNDS

PROMINENT MARKS
R.D #2 Box 19, Shamokin, Penna.

COUNTERSIGNED: _____
GPO   16—37087-1   RECRUITING OFFICER.

Although Jack left high school about three months before his scheduled graduation, he did receive his diploma. His name was read at the commencement ceremony and a senior girl accepted his diploma for him. The diploma was then delivered to Jack's mother.

9753

FROM

JACK   LAWRENCE   McSHERRY,   JR   Company No. _3102_
First Name   Middle Name   Last Name

U. S. NAVAL TRAINING CENTER, BAINBRIDGE, MARYLAND.

TO   Mr.
   (Mrs.) _Ivy L. McSHERRY_
   Miss

Street and No. _R.D.#2   Box 19_

City _SHAMOKIN_   State _PENNA._

Nearest Express Office _____

Upon arriving at the Bainbridge Naval Base, Jack was issued his navy uniform and accessories. He, therefore, packed his civilian clothes into a carton and mailed them home to his mother.

The kid is now in the United States Navy.

Chapter II

BOOT CAMP

At the Naval Training Station in Bainbridge, Maryland, the first thing that the new recruits received was a haircut. Most of them had the hair cut down to about 1/8" above the scalp. They were then referred to as "skinheads".

Jack was assigned to Company 3107 in the Third Regiment. Company 3107 occupied the second floor of the barracks. Their bunks were lined up side by side, filling up the floor area of the barracks. At the foot of the bunk, each person had a wooden chest in which they kept their clothing and other personal items.

Company 3107 was commanded by Chief Petty Officer Hanna, who was a very likeable man. Everyone in the Company liked Chief Hanna, so whatever he told them to do, they did it cheerfully and without hesitation. The first things that the new recruits learned was how to make up their bunks, then they learned how to fold their uniforms so they could store them in their chest without causing them to wrinkle. They learned how to roll their socks into a compact unit.

Reveille was sounded at 5:00 AM and everyone jumped out of their bunks and proceeded immediately into the head (nautical for restroom) to wash up, shave, brush their teeth, comb their hair, if they had any, and prepare for the day's activities.

Each of them proceeded to their assigned cleaning stations to thoroughly clean the barracks. Some cleaned the decks (the floor), others cleaned the head, and other areas and surfaces of the barracks. Jack was assigned to clean a certain two windows in the barracks. Each morning, he would wash the two windows, inside and outside, then proceed to dry them into a totally clean state using portions of newspapers. The barracks was cleaned in this manner every morning before breakfast.

The

Bluejackets' Manual

UNITED STATES NAVY

1944

Twelfth Edition

United States Naval Institute
Annapolis, Maryland
1944

Each recruit received a copy
of the Bluejacket's Manual.

After thoroughly cleaning the barracks, the Company would go down the stairway and to the outside in front of the barracks. There they would stand in formation for roll call and to receive the agenda for the day. In addition to being told what they would be doing all day, certain names would be called telling these people that they must report to the Camp Dentist at a certain time that day. That was frightening to Jack, because when he was a little kid his mother took him to the dentist to have some cavities drilled and repaired. At that time dental work was extremely painful and Jack suffered through it. He never wanted to see a dentist again after that experience. Every day at the roll call and briefing, Jack shook in horror that his name would be called to see the dentist. Finally, his name was called and he had to go to the dentist. Obediently, he went to the dentist. The dentist, a Lieutenant Commander, filled all of Jack's cavities and caused him absolutely no pain. Jack was relieved and very happy.

After the roll call and reception of the day's agenda, the Company marched in formation from the barracks to the mess hall for breakfast. In the mess hall, they lined up and proceeded to the food counter where they each picked up a metal tray and the utensils. Then they passed in front of the food counter while holding their trays out toward the counter. There the merciless personnel behind the counter would slam various food items onto the tray with very little finesse. Upon receiving portions of all the food being offered, the individuals would proceed to the mess hall tables, sit down, and enjoy their food. Coffee was always provided for every meal.

The agenda each day was something different. The recruits were taught how to handle a rifle, and to perform the orders of arms, which were the ceremonious procedures of presenting the arms.

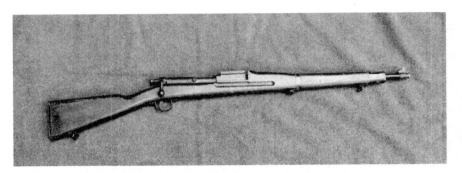

The wooden rifle carried by the recruits

They were sent to the drill field to form up and to learn how to march and to perform all of the procedures of marching in formation while carrying a wooden rifle. This marching and drilling went on all day, and at that time of the year, the temperature was in the 90's. The Company did their drilling and did it well.

They were given gas masks to wear, then they were sent into a concrete structure containing several rooms. Then tear gas was sent into the room. They were told to remove their gas masks so they could see the difference in the gas filled room with the masks on and with masks off. They removed their masks and were then allowed to leave the room as fast as they could to get away from the gas. The eyes burned for a while after this event.

They were sent to another concrete structure where they were provided with fire-fighting equipment. Then oil was set on fire inside the structure, and with the assistance of a qualified instructor, they were sent into the structure to put out the fire.

Another assignment was to enter a classroom, be seated, and shown silhouettes of aircraft, friendly as well as enemy aircraft. The different aircraft were shown and differences and outstanding features of the various aircraft were discussed. After going over these features, various aircraft silhouettes were flashed onto a screen and the class was asked to shout out the identity of the plane. Jack performed very poorly in this procedure. He seemed to think that all of them were Japanese Bettys, a Japanese bomber.

This is the type slides that were used in the training classes for the recruits to learn to identify the various aircraft involved in the war. This particular slide is for the identification of the Japanese "Betty".

When projected to the screen, this is an example of what had to be identified. The plane shown on this projection is the Japanese Betty.

After attending the aircraft recognition school, the company was sent to an area for physical training. (Most of the men termed it physical torture). Even though Jack weighed only 129 pounds at the time, he was in good physical condition and very flexible, so the physical torture was not a problem for him. The instructor sat on a chair on a wooden platform and gave orders for different physical exercises that the Company should do. He would count the exercises off as he sat comfortably on his chair. Jack could do the push-ups as required, and the jumping jacks, and the chin-ups, but many of the men, some as old as thirty years, had difficulties keeping up.

One of the days, they were sent to a site that had a large anti-aircraft gun. They took turns manning the various positions to shoot the gun. There was a man to lift the projectile from its standby location, pass it on to another who handed it to the man that would slide it into the rear of the gun barrel. Then the gun was fired and immediately the large brass casing of the projectile would be ejected out of the barrel at the rear of the gun. This casing was to be caught by a man and thrown aside. Of course, they were firing blanks. This exercise was fun, but it was also a little scary.

On several occasions, the Company would be taken to the obstacle course where they would run through it as fast as possible with many obstacles to slow them down. For Jack, running the obstacle course was easy and fun. The older guys had a tough time. One of the items on the obstacle course, which Jack enjoyed, was a horizontal ladder, about twenty feet long and about eight or nine feet off the ground. He watched the thirty year old guys struggle to move from rung to rung, then when they cleared the ladder, Jack jumped up and grabbed the first rung. He then swung his body and reached out and grabbed the third or fourth rung, and continued in that manner to the other end.

Most of these programs were visited by the Company many times during the term of the boot training. Especially the marching drill, the physical torture and the obstacle course.

While in boot camp, Jack was in the third regiment. George Miller, who enlisted with jack, was in the fifth regiment, so Jack applied for permits to visit George in the fifth regiment. He made two visits to George. Once on May 6 and again on May 13.

During all of this training in boot camp, Jack was in a company with many older men, late twenties to early thirties. Strangely enough, many of these men were contracting childhood diseases, like measles, mumps, and chicken pox. They would then be sent to the hospital where they stayed until cured.

One hot day, the temperature went up to about 105 degrees while Company 3107 was marching around the drill field, carrying their wooden rifles. While doing this, Jack's throat got sorer and sorer and his head felt hotter and hotter. He didn't say anything. He figured it was just a temporary inconvenience, so he marched on and on. At about 5:00 in the afternoon, the Company marched back to their barracks. In the barracks, while standing alongside his bunk, Jack was taking his tee shirt off in preparation for taking a nice cold shower. As he removed the tee shirt, the man in the bunk next to him, when he saw Jack's bright red chest, proclaimed that Jack had scarlet fever and should go to the sick bay. Jack went to the sick bay and was diagnosed with scarlet fever. They sent him to the base hospital. In the hospital, a crotchety old doctor came to see him and he told him that he would knock that scarlet fever right out of him. He told Jack that he will give him a double shot of penicillin.

He leaned Jack across a desk and gave him a double dose of penicillin in the seat. Penicillin was a new medicine at that time. The double dose of penicillin knocked the scarlet fever out of Jack just as the Doctor said it would. In three days, Jack was discharged from the hospital and sent to a recuperating barracks for several days. Then he was sent back to his Company.

Finally, after twelve weeks, boot camp was completed and all of the members of Company 3107 graduated. While in boot camp, everyone was rated as an apprentice seaman. When they graduated, they were advanced in rank to Seaman second class.

Upon graduating from boot camp, everyone got a seven day leave except Jack. Jack was scheduled to start quartermaster school immediately after boot camp. The quartermaster school was in another area of the Bainbridge Naval Station.

While in quartermaster school, Jack usually went home for the weekends. His customary means of transportation was to take a bus from the Naval Base to the train station in Lancaster. From Lancaster, he took a train to Harrisburg. Then he would hitchhike from Harrisburg to Tharptown. However, sometimes he would take the train from Lancaster to Sunbury, then hitchhike from Sunbury to Tharptown.

In Quartermaster school, Jack learned navigation, signaling, and the other requirements necessary to perform the work of the Quartermaster. The best job on the ship is to be a quartermaster. On a ship, the quartermaster stood the quartermaster watch on the bridge, he wrote the ships log, he assisted the Navigator with the navigation procedures, and he was an expert helmsman. He always knew where the ship was, where she was going, and what was going on. It was an excellent job.

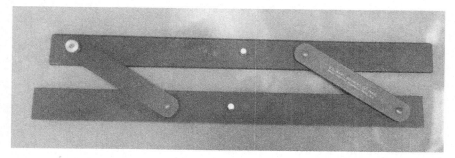

This parallel rule is the type used in navigation in the World War 2 era. They were used to transfer parallel lines on the navigation charts.

U.S. NAVY, BUSHIPS (N) 1943.
PARK INST. CO., ROCHELLE PARK, N.J.

This is the inscription on the parallel rule which shows the Navy, Manufacturer, and date.

Just as there are laws governing the procedures and requirements for driving a car, there are Rules of the Road for ships at sea. There are the Rules of the Road for navigating in the Inland Waters, which are the Bays and other areas near the land masses, and for traffic out at sea, there are the International Rules of the Road. Sometimes these Rules differ with each other, but usually they are the same for Inland Waters and International Waters.

One example of the International Rules of the Road is if two ships are traveling toward each other at right angles and are on a collision course, the ship to the starboard (right) side of the other has the right of way and may maintain his speed and direction. The other ship must give a blast on his whistle, change course or slow down to give way to the ship with the right of way.

When traveling in fog, In accordance with the International Rules of the Road, a ship must blow the whistle for four to six seconds on intervals of not more than two minutes.

In addition, these Rules also provide detailed requirements for the lighting of the ships. A green light is on the starboard side of the ship and a red light on the port side of the ship. There are running lights on the masts of the ships. Following are some examples of the lighting, however, the colors of the lights do not show up on the black and white photograph.

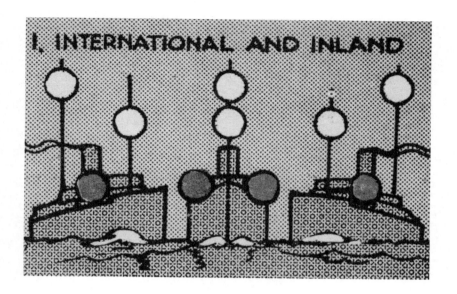

Signaling from one ship to another, to send messages, several different visual methods existed. There was the morse code which was used with flashing lights, The semaphore was by using two hand-held flags in which each position of the flags was a different letter of the alphabet. Then there were signal flags which were flown on the yardarm of the mast.

Some of the signal flags are shown as follows:

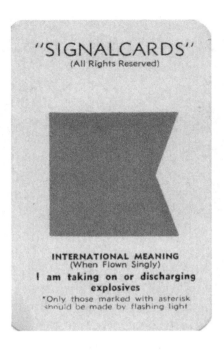

B called "Baker". This flag is totally red in color, and when flown alone on the yardarm of a ship it indicates that the ship is in the process of taking on, or discharging, explosives. It could indicate other dangerous operations in addition.

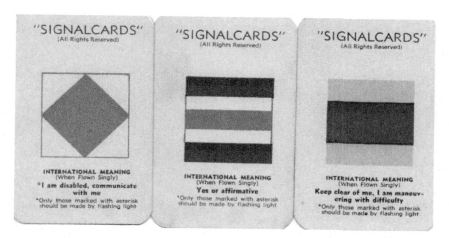

These flags are F called "Fox", C called "Charlie", and D called "Dog". If one of these flags is flown alone on the yardarm, it has the meaning as printed on the card. However, if these three flags are flown together as FCD, in accordance with the International signal flag code, it means to "Begin present operations". When the operations are to end, the D is removed and replaced with a J. FCJ means "cease present operations".

A tradition at sea, but not an international regulation, was for a merchant ship, when passing in the presence of a Man Of War (a warship), would dip her national flag to acknowledge the presence of the warship. This was not a requirement but was a courtesy. As she approached the warship, the merchant ship would lower her flag to half mast. The warship would acknowledge this courtesy by lowering her flag to half mast then immediately return it to the top of the mast. The merchant ship would then raise her flag back to the top of the mast. The response to the dip would be performed by the Quartermaster of the watch on the warship.

Upon graduating from quartermaster school, Jack was promoted to seaman first class.

Jack McSherry, Jr., David McSherry, Jack McSherry, Bill McSherry World War II

Jack was then sent to Newport, Rhode Island where he was assigned, as a transient, to a bunk in a metal Quonset hut. This was in the wintertime and the hut was heated by a coal stove. While there, one night Jack was assigned to stand the mid-watch, midnight to four in the morning, in an isolated area among some unoccupied Quonset huts. He went to the area a little before midnight and relieved the person who was presently standing the watch. The man turned his rifle over to Jack. Jack slung the rifle over his shoulder and began walking around the area. Jack carried that rifle around for hours and saw no one. The area was totally isolated. At 3:45 AM, Jack was supposed to be relieved by someone else. As of 5:00 AM, no one showed up to relieve him, so, after hiking around the area for over five hours, and seeing no-one, Jack concluded that he spent enough time walking around that desolate area. He leaned his rifle against a building and went back to his Quonset hut and went to bed. Having been on the mid-watch, he was allowed to sleep in his bunk until noon, which he did. No one ever asked any questions about the watch, or about the rifle and there were never any repercussions.

When Jack enlisted in the Navy, he signed up as a reserve V-6, which is the way that most enlistees signed up. This enlistment was for the period of time until both Germany and Japan surrendered, plus six months. On November 3, 1945, while on the Naval Base at Newport, Jack reenlisted into the regular Navy on a minority enlistment. A minority enlistment is when a seventeen year old enlists to be discharged on the day before his 21st birthday. So Jack was discharged from the Navy reserve and was enlisted into the regular Navy.

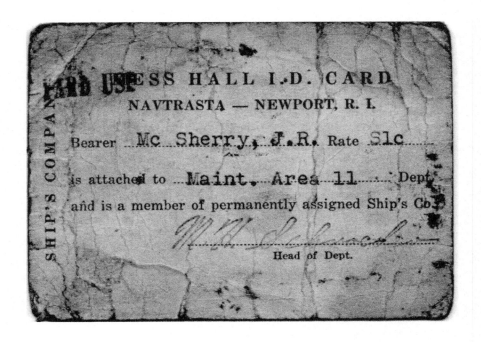

MESS HALL I.D. CARD

NAVTRASTA — NEWPORT, R. I.

Bearer Mc Sherry, J.R. Rate S1c

is attached to Maint. Area 11 Dept.

and is a member of permanently assigned Ship's Co.

Head of Dept.

After some time as a transient on the Newport Naval Base, Jack was assigned to go aboard the USS Houston, CL-81, a light cruiser which was anchored in the Narraganset Bay.

On the Houston, Jack performed the work of a quartermaster including steering the ship. The Houston left the Narragansett Bay and cruised around in the North Atlantic. This area was considered a war area, so Jack received his American Campaign medal.

After about five weeks on the Houston, on February 22, 1946, the ship got underway and went to the Philadelphia navy yard. Jack was then transferred to the USS Huntington which was moored to the dock in the navy Yard. The Huntington was a new ship, a light cruiser, which was only recently launched and was still not a commissioned ship of the Navy. Jack went aboard the ship and the next day they held the commissioning ceremonies and the ship became a commissioned ship of the Navy. At the ceremonies for the commissioning, Jack's job was to raise the American flag to the top of the mast for the first time. When the flag went up the mast, she became a commissioned ship of the Navy.

COMMISSIONING CEREMONY

Prospective Executive Officer--Orders "Attention" on the bugle.

Prospective Commanding Officer--"Admiral Draemel, we are ready to proceed with the commissioning".

Admiral Draemel--"Very Well. We will now proceed with the commissioning ceremony. Chaplain _____ give the Invocation".

Prospective Executive Officer--"HUNTINGTON Crew, Uncover. Two".

Chaplain _____ delivers the Invocation.

Prospective Executive Officer--"Cover, Two. Parade Rest".

Admiral Draemel--Delivers address. Reads commissioning directive. Directs "Captain Tallman, Place the ship in commission".

Captain Tallman to Commander Wilson--"Place the ship in commission".

Commander Wilson to Captain Tallman--"Aye, Aye, Sir. HUNTINGTON Crew attention. All divisions face aft. Sound off".

Ship is placed in commission

Commander Wilson to Captain Tallman--"Captain, the U.S.S. HUNTINGTON has been placed in commission".

Captain Tallman--Reads his orders.

Captain Tallman to Admiral Draemel--"Admiral Draemel, I accept command of the U.S.S. HUNTINGTON".

Captain Tallman to Commander Wilson--"Break the Admiral's Flag".

Commander Wilson to Captain Tallman--"Aye, Aye, Sir".

Commander Wilson--"Break the Flag of Admiral Draemel".

Honors rendered by band and crew.

Captain Tallman to Commander Wilson--"Commander Wilson, set the watch".

Commander Wilson to Captain Tallman--"Aye, Aye, Sir".

Commander Wilson to Chief Boatswain Garner--"Boatswain, set the watch, First Section. Commander Gregor, you have the first watch as Officer-of-the-Deck".

Commander Wilson to crew--"Parade Rest".

Captain Tallman delivers address. Introduces distinguished guests.

Commander Gregor to Commander Wilson--"Sir, the watch has been set".

Commander Wilson to Commander Gregor—"Very well".

Commander Wilson to Captain Tallman—"Sir, the Watch has been set".

Captain Tallman—"Very well".

Captain Tallman to Chaplain Huff—"Chaplain, pronounce the Benediction".

Commander Wilson to Crew—"HUNTINGTON Crew, Attention. Uncover, Two".

Chaplain Huff pronounces benediction.

Commander Wilson to Crew—"HUNTINGTON Crew, Cover. Two".

Captain Tallman to Commander Wilson—"Pipe down".

Commander Wilson to Captain Tallman—"Aye, Aye, Sir".

Commander Wilson to Commander Gregor—"Secure from commissioning ceremony".

Commander Gregor to Bugler—"Sound attention".

Commander Gregor to Boatswain's Mate-of-the-Watch—"Pipe down".

Boatswain-of-the-Watch pipes down.

Commander Wilson to guests—You are cordially invited on board".

Commander Gregor to Bugler—"Sound Retreat".

Bugler sounds "Retreat".

Commander Wilson—"Division Officers take charge and dismiss your
divisions".

About two weeks later, the Huntington left the Philadelphia Navy Yard, cruised down the Delaware River to the Atlantic Ocean, and headed for Guantanamo Bay, Cuba on her shakedown cruise. Being out to sea and cruising along the east coast of the United States was very exciting to Jack.

CHAPTER III

AT SEA

As the USS Huntington approached the island of Cuba, from a distance, the outline of the land was silhouetted against the sky and appeared almost black. As the ship came closer to the land, the color of the land changed to green. Before long, being closer, the vegetation became totally visible.

USS Huntington CL-107

On April 4, 1946, the ship entered the harbor of Guantanamo. Navigation into the harbor was conducted by the Navigator, with the quartermasters shooting angles on the lighthouses and other geographical structures. To make the entry easier and providing great assistance to the navigation, there were range masts in line on the shore whereby the ship would steer directly toward them, keeping them on a straight line up to a certain point, then turn right to a predetermined location where they dropped anchor, having arrived in the naval Base at Guantanamo.

The next day, Jack, along with several friends, went ashore on liberty. Liberty at Guantanamo was different than most other ports. Guantanamo was a Naval Base. The main attraction to the ship's crew was the Beer Tent which was located on the beach area close to the crew's dropping off point from the liberty boat. The beer served was named "Hatuey" beer, and the label on the beer contained a picture of an Indian. Most of the crew spent the entire afternoon and evening in that tent.

Jack did not drink any alcoholic beverages, so after observing the beer tent, he and his friends walked a little further to the base's swimming pool, where they enjoyed themselves swimming. They then returned to the dock, got on the liberty boat and returned to the ship. That was the extent of liberty at Guantanamo.

However, after several liberties on the Naval base, Jack, usually by himself, began hiking around the base to see what else was there. Barracks and such buildings are not very exciting, so he hiked along the shoreline over the sandy beach and observed the nature of the ocean. Liberty after liberty, Jack hiked and hiked, enjoying the desert-like land.

Although the sailors were prohibited from crossing the border between the naval Base and the Land of Cuba, this one Sunday afternoon, Jack decided to explore the land adjacent to the Naval Base. There was no fence at the border nor any guards. It was apparently assumed by the Government that no one would want to walk into the hot desert land beyond.

Jack walked into Cuba, observing the sand and the cactus. He first hiked along the shoreline, but then turned inland. As he hiked along, the scenery was always the same, sand and cactus. Even though it sounds monotonous, Jack enjoyed every minute of his hike. Eventually, he came upon an apparently abandoned old church with a small cemetery alongside it. Much to Jack's excitement one of the tombstones in the cemetery contained the name, "Frank McSherry, died 1749". Frank McSherry was apparently a distant relative of Jack's.

Jack continued his hike. Having hiked several miles in the desert in the hot sun, it happens that Jack never once thought of the need to get a drink of water. It was in Jack's nature that he never did develop a thirst.

Jack continued his hike. He enjoyed walking through the desert, but nothing changed. There were no houses, no roads, nor anything other than sand and cactus.

Finally after hiking for quite a few hours, Jack decided to head back to the naval Base. The return trip to the base was about the same as the trip into the desert, sand and cactus. When Jack got to about 200 feet from the border between Cuba and the Base, he was confronted by a United States Marine carrying a rifle. The Marine asked Jack what he was doing 200 feet on the wrong side of the border. Jack responded with the innocent statement, "Oh, am I over the border?" To which the marine responded, "Yes you are, get back over to the Base where you belong." Obediently, Jack crossed over the border into the Base, and all was well. Jack did not tell the marine that he had about a ten mile hike into and back out of Cuba.

On regular intervals, the Huntington would go out to sea to conduct training exercises of some sort. The ship practiced approaching another ship, connecting up tow lines, and proceeding to tow the other vessel. Another exercise at sea was to go alongside a tanker, run a hose between the tanker and the Huntington and refuel the ship.

Groups of ships met, went into formation and maneuvered as a fleet. Maneuvering with this fleet, the Huntington went past Haiti and Jamaica. Enroute, the Huntington travelled alongside other ships, connected up hoses and refueled the other ships from the Huntington's fuel tanks. The ship passed by Puerto Rico, and anchored off Culebra Island. For several weeks, the ships maneuvered around the area of Culebra Island and Vieques Island, practicing gunfire while at general quarters. The USS Huntington and the USS Missouri practiced bombarding the shoreline with their large guns. The ship practiced taking on supplies from other ships while cruising at sea.

The Huntington left the area of Culeba Island and headed for San Juan, Puerto Rico where they moored to the dock. In the city of San Juan, Jack walked the streets and the countryside. Everything was new and different to him. There were palm trees, very different architecture, the El Morro Castle and a strange language.

El Morro Castle, San Juan, Puerto Rico
May 1946

After several days in San Juan, the Huntington returned to Guantanamo Bay. Every several days the ship would leave Guantanamo and maneuver around in the sea, practicing the many duties and needs of the ship.

On June 1, 1946, Jack was promoted to Quartermaster third class.

For the remainder of the month of June, the Huntington maneuvered near Guantanamo Bay. The gun crews had considerable practice shooting their anti- aircraft guns at drones flying in the sky. Drones are unmanned, radio controlled planes. The gunner's instructions were to shoot close to the drones but do not hit them. The Huntington gunners did well. The gunshot was with 20 Millimeter guns, 40 millimeter guns, and 5" guns.

On June 28, 1946, the activities for training on the shakedown cruise were completed and the Huntington got underway from the Naval Base at Guantanamo Bay enroute to the Philadelphia Navy yard.

On the cruise back to the United States, the ship followed the commercial channels off the east coast. At one point in this travel, the orders were given to increase the speed of the ship from the normal cruise speed of 15 knots to flank speed. Flank speed supposedly is the maximum speed that the ship can do. The speed was increased until the ship was cutting the water at a speed of 33 knots. As the ship moved through the commercial channel, they overtook several commercial ships which were travelling at the speed of ten knots. This created excitement not only on the Huntington, but on the passed ships also. It was like driving a car and passing all of the other cars on the road.

The term "knots" is misunderstood and misused by many people, so that will be cleared up here. A knot is a velocity. A knot is a nautical mile per hour. A nautical mile is 6000 feet.

As the Huntington cruised northward. Every night Jack slept in his bunk in the living quarters of the ship.

Bunks were placed three high throughout the living quarters. Jack slept in a top bunk adjacent to the outside bulkhead of the ship. As he laid in his bunk, which was about fifteen feet below the surface of the ocean, he could hear the seawater rushing alongside the bulkhead. Also, he could hear the bulkhead buckling back and forth as it was under the stress of water pressure variations on the outside. It thumped rather loudly each time that it buckled. Jack didn't say anything to anyone because it did not concern him. Jack knew that ships were not built to sink. When the ship returned to the Philadelphia Navy Yard, she was put in dry-dock and the hull was examined. While there, they welded some steel angle irons to the bulkhead in the area adjacent to Jack's bunk as reinforcement. Apparently someone other than Jack noticed the buckling of the bulkhead.

Cruising northward along the East coast of the United States, the Huntington arrived at the mouth of the Delaware River on July 1. 1946. The cruise up the river took a little over seven hours. She moored to the dock later that morning at 10:20.

Upon mooring to the dock in the Navy Yard, the flag of Rear Admiral E. W. Burroughs was raised to the top of the mast of the Huntington. Thus, with Admiral Burroughs aboard, the Huntington became the flagship for Cruiser Division Twelve, of the Atlantic Fleet.

CHAPTER IV

CRUISES TO THE MEDITERRANEAN SEA

On July 23, 1946, the Huntington got underway from the Philadelphia Navy Yard enroute to Naples, Italy. The ocean was calm and the cruise across the Atlantic was very pleasant and very interesting, especially to a young teenager.

Other than standing his quartermaster watches on the bridge, Jack was assigned another duty. For a certain period of time, he was to wind all the clocks on the ship, of which there were about fifty of them. He wound clocks on the bridge, in the mess hall, the engine room, the officer's wardroom, and in every nook and cranny on the ship. His favorite clock to wind was in the Admiral's stateroom.

Jack would knock on the Admiral's door. The door would be opened and Jack was greeted and invited in by the Admiral. He would then wind the Admiral's clock. Doing this every day, they came to a point where they would make conversation. The Admiral and Jack, even though the Admiral was at the top of the ranking and Jack was near the bottom, became friendly acquaintances. Obviously Admiral Burroughs took a liking to Jack and perpetuated the unusual friendship.

Jack and the Admiral were friends in a strange way, because it was not proper for an Admiral and a third class Quartermaster to be friends.

On one occasion, while Jack was on watch on the quarterdeck while the ship was tied up to the dock,

The officer of the deck noticed the union jack, which was flying at the staff on the bow of the ship, was sagging several inches from the top of the staff. The officer of the deck told Jack to go to the bow and "two block" the flag. He proceeded to do that. On his way back to the quarterdeck, he walked past the Admiral who happened to be standing along his route. Jack stopped and talked to him briefly, then went to the quarterdeck. When he got back, the officer of the deck, Ensign Bellinger, was in a rage and bawled him out for talking to the Admiral. Jack told him that they talk all the time. Ensign Bellinger, being a mere ensign would never be allowed to talk to the Admiral without being invited. Apparently that bothered him a little.

On August 2, 1946, the Huntington passed through the strait of Gibraltar. The Rock of Gibraltar was only about five miles to the left of the ship as she steamed by, giving the crew of the ship a very good view of the Rock.

Continuing eastward into the Mediterranean Sea, the Huntington cruised through the blue waters of the Mediterranean Sea for several days. On August 5, she entered the harbor at Naples, passed by the volcano Vesuvius, and moored alongside the USS Fargo, CL 106, a sister ship of the Huntington and a unit of the twelfth Cruiser Division. The Fargo was moored to a dock. This dock was not the commonly recognized dock, but it was actually a capsized Italian Cruiser laying on her side in the harbor, a casualty of World War II. The gangways from the ships that were tied to this "dock" were lowered onto the side of the cruiser and lined up with a wooden walkway attached to the cruiser which led to the real dock several hundred feet away.

During the ship's stay in the Mediterranean, Naples was the home base for the Huntington. The capsized Italian cruiser was the dock that she always tied up to whenever she was in Naples.

Naples, Italy, August 6, 1946

The day after arriving in Naples, the Huntington got underway for the free city of Trieste. This cruise headed south from Naples toward the Strait of Messina which is between the southern end of the Italian mainland and Sicily. Just before reaching the Strait, the ship passed by Stromboli, a live volcano located to the right of the ship. This Volcano was unusual in that it was a round, conical island with smoke and steam flowing out of its top.

A short distance beyond Stromboli, the ship entered the Strait of Messina. After cruising a short distance into the Strait, the Volcano Mount Etna, could be seen to the right of the ship in Sicily. This was also an active Volcano.

The ship passed through the Strait of Messina, passed around the Southern tip of Italy, then proceeded northward, in the Adriatic Sea, along the east coast of Italy. The Huntington moored to the dock in Trieste on August 8, 1946.

Trieste was a free city in 1946. Both Italy and Yugoslavia claimed it as their own. As a result, there was considerable unrest and rioting in and around Trieste at that time. Possibly as a symbol of authority, when the Huntington was moored to the dock, the bow of the ship was directed toward the downtown plaza of Trieste. With the ship in this position, the ship's 6" gun turret was aimed at the plaza.

This was the ship's first visit to Trieste. Through the rest of August, the ship remained in Trieste. The ship's crew was granted liberty to go ashore every second day. Jack took advantage of that.

On one of the first liberties into the city, Jack and his friends were walking up the street looking for an acceptable restaurant. It happened that they saw Admiral Burroughs and his aides walking up the street some distance ahead of them. As they followed at a distance, before long, the Admiral and his group went into a restaurant. Jack's group waited a reasonable time, then entered the same restaurant, which was a very nice, high class restaurant. Jack had a very good dishful of Italian Spaghetti. They liked the restaurant and went there many more times thereafter.

Over many of Jack's liberties into Trieste, he hiked all over the City, as was his procedure during all of his travels through the countries of the Mediterranean.

On August 20, 1946, the ship got underway from Trieste and headed for Venice, Italy. Nine hours later, they arrived in Venice. The ship proceeded into the harbor at Venice, turned into the Grand Canal, and after going a sort distance, made a U-turn and moored to the dock a few hundred feet from Saint Mark's Square.

The USS Huntington entering the Grand Canal

Venice and the Grand Canal, August 20, 1946

That evening, Jack and his friends went ashore and observed with amazement the many bridges and canals. There was no other place in the world like Venice. They walked through St. Mark's Square, observed Saint Mark's Cathedral, and the many other famous structures in that Square. They then walked through the mazes of walkways along the canals throughout the town. The gondolas and many other traffic boats were cruising up and down the canal. How could anything be more exciting than this?

St. Mark's Cathedral, Venice, Italy
August 23, 1946

Six days later, the Huntington got underway from Venice and returned to Trieste. Jack took all advantages to go ashore whenever possible and hiked the streets. Everything was different than back home.

While at Trieste, the ship went out to sea to locate a reported floating mine. In the late afternoon, the mine was located. The mine was destroyed by shooting it with the ship's 40 millimeter guns.

During the ship's time in Trieste, Jack went ashore every time he had the chance. He walked around town and observed whatever was there to see. At that time, the Italians and the Yugoslavs were fighting over the city. Each country wanted possession of it. The boundary between Trieste and Yugoslavia was called the Morgan line. At a briefing in the mess hall shortly after their arrival in Trieste, the crew was told about the situation in Trieste, and how to conduct themselves while on shore. They were told not to cross the Morgan line.

Everywhere that Jack went, it was his custom to walk throughout the city that they were visiting, and often beyond the bounds of the city. One Sunday afternoon as he was walking around in the streets of Trieste all by himself, he headed into the countryside. He enjoyed himself walking along dirt roads and observing the sights. Sometimes he took shortcuts across fields, but always observant of his surroundings. After walking for quite some time, things looked a little different. He was in Yugoslavia!

He had crossed the Morgan Line. It was interesting, but he decided to return to Trieste, so he walked back across the Morgan line and on into Trieste. No one knew that he had been in Yugoslavia, and all was well.

However, one day in 1975, Jack was watching a documentary on television with his son, Jack III. To Jack's excitement, it was about Trieste and the problems of 1946. Jack Recognized areas and called out, "I was there". Jack's interest was peaking when the narrator mentioned that they are just now clearing the Morgan line of mines. That is where he became surprised because he never knew that the Morgan Line was mined. Somehow, he apparently missed the mines when he walked through the area, both ways. Jack complained that, at the briefing in the mess hall, they told everyone not to cross the Morgan Line, they did not say why!

On September 11, 1946, The Huntington got underway from Trieste, passed through the Strait of Messina and moored to the dock at Naples on September 14, 1946. While moored to the dock in Naples, Jack and his friends took a train to Pompeii. This was another fantastic, historical visit. They walked the streets of Pompeii, observing the deep ruts in the stones of the street caused by all of the chariot wheels passing back and forth during the heyday of Pompeii.

 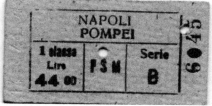

For those who do not know the history of Pompeii, the town was totally destroyed by being covered over by hot ashes from the eruption of Mount Vesuvius in the year 29 AD. Only a few buildings remained standing, and very few people survived the disaster.

Jack and his group observed the remains of the buildings along the street. In several cases, they were able to go inside a few houses. There were paintings on the walls, painted directly onto the plastered wall. The group went into the remains of the Arena, where many of the bleachers for the observers are still standing, where the people sat to watch the event occurring in the great arena space below.

While moored to the dock in Naples, an Italian artist came aboard the ship and displayed many oil paintings on the tables in the mess hall. They were for sale. Jack purchased one of a frigate at sea, which was painted by L. Papaluca. Jack still has that painting.

A black and white copy of the Papaluca painting

The artist, Roberto Maresca, told the crew members that he could paint portraits of people from photographs if anyone was interested. Jack happened to have a very small picture of his grandfather in his wallet, a picture that he had taken, developed, and printed himself. This picture was only about an inch wide and one and a half inches high. Jack gave the picture, along with his home address, to the artist to paint

Original Photo

Oil Painting of Grandfather

The picture arrived at Jack's home after several months, but Jack was still cruising around in the Mediterranean. When he got home on leave, he opened the package and pulled out the portrait. The painting measures about 14" x 18". Jack drove to his Grandfather's home in Bear Gap, Pennsylvania, to show him the portrait. Grandfather got very excited about the portrait and asked Jack if it was for him.

That was not Jack's intention, but he could not say no, so he gave it to his Grandfather. Then Grandfather gave a photograph of Jack's Grandmother to Jack. Jack sent the picture to Mr. Maresca and ordered a companion portrait for his Grandfather. Mr. Maresca painted a companion portrait and mailed it to Jack. Jack gave the portrait of Grandmother to his Grandfather, who hung them side by side in his living room.

Oil Painting of Grandmother

Original Photo

Jack's Grandfather, David H. Burrell, died in 1951, but the portraits continued to hang side by side in the living room. In the year 1992, the last of Jack's uncles David F. Burrell, died. David F. Burrell lived in that same house from his birth in 1909 until his death in 1992. When David F. Burrell died, Jack again received custody of the portraits of his Grandparents. Those portraits are now hanging on the wall in Jack's house.

On September 23, 1946, the Huntington left Naples in company with the USS Fargo and the destroyers, USS Corry and the USS New. The ships passed through the Strait of Messina. They then proceeded to the waters around the Island of Malta where they dropped anchor.

The next morning, the Huntington left Malta and anchored in the Naples Harbor briefly, then again raised anchor and got underway for Leghorn, Italy. The Italian name for Leghorn is Livorno. The next afternoon, the ship arrived in Livorno and anchored in the outer harbor. The town of Livorno did not exist anymore as a result of the bombardments of World War II. The town consisted of brick rubble and little more. The harbor was cluttered with sunken ships. The water was rather shallow in the harbor so that the sunken ships, although resting on the bottom of the harbor, were extending above the water level with their masts going high into the air.

The next day, Jack and his friend Herbert Miller, went ashore on liberty. They walked across what used to be the town of Livorno and came to a highway that was going north. They used the method of transportation known as hitchhiking to try to go to

Pisa. The hitchhiking was successful, and they ended up at the southern end of the town of Pisa. They walked northward through the town to the north end of the town where they found the leaning tower of Pisa. Upon arriving at the tower, they walked up the stone stairway which wound circularly around the perimeter of the inside of the tower. At the top of the stairway, they walked out onto the stone deck of the top of the tower. The floor sloped the same as the tower sloped.

Jack and Herb Miller At the leaning tower of Pisa
September 29, 1946

Jack walked around on the top of the tower and looked in all directions. The entire town of Pisa was visible on the one side. Open lands were visible in the distance, and upon looking straight down, the tops of tourist's heads were visible. Another thing that fascinated Jack was that he probably stood in the exact location where Galileo made his famous experiment by dropping a brick and a half-brick to the ground below. Both the brick and the half-brick hit the ground at the same time, proving that weight is not a factor in the speed of a falling object.

The two of them then descended the stairway to the ground below. They walked across the street to a walkway lined with souvenir stores. The one store is where they carved and sold objects of alabaster. Jack saw a small horse carved from alabaster. Knowing that his Uncle Calvin, back in the United States, liked horses, Jack bought the horse for Uncle Calvin.

The next time that he went home he gave the horse to Uncle Calvin, who appreciated the gift very much. Uncle Calvin put the horse on a small shelf on his Mother's sideboard in the dining room. The horse remained in that location from that time forward. Uncle Calvin died in 1956, but the horse remained in the same location. When Calvin's younger brother, David, died in 1992, Jack again received ownership of the horse. At that same time, jack purchased the sideboard at a family auction. The horse is now standing on the same shelf, on the same sideboard in Jack's house.

This is a photo of Grandmother's sideboard
with the alabaster horse on the shelf.

Fifty eight years later, in 2004, Jack again visited the Leaning Tower of Pisa. After climbing the tower and making his observations, he crossed the street and went into the alabaster shop, which was still there. After some conversation with one of the matronly ladies who worked there, it was revealed that she worked in that shop in 1946 when Jack purchased the horse. When he left the shop, he told the lady that he would see her again in 58 years. She smiled, and was pleased.

While in Livorno, Jack took a short journey to Florence where he looked around the City. He stayed overnight in a hotel in Florence. The next day, he returned to the ship.

Florence, Italy, October 1, 1946

On October 3, 1946, The USS Huntington left Livorno and headed for Genoa, Italy. Eight hours later, the ship moored to the dock at Genoa.

Jack went on liberty into the town of Genoa. As soon as he left the ship he came to a very large statue of Christopher Columbus. The inscription on the statue said, "Cristoforo Colombo, La Patria". Every time that Jack was in Genoa and went into town, he walked past that statue.

Genoa was a nice town and quite interesting. Jack saw the house in which Columbus was supposedly born.

The Columbus Monument
Genoa, Italy, October, 1946

When in port, the Officer of the Deck would stand his watches on the quarterdeck. Along with the officer of the deck, there would be a quartermaster, boatswains mate, and a messenger. For those standing the mid-watch, which was from midnight to four in the morning, it was customary for the baker to have some kind of goodie that these people could pick up in the mess hall along with a cup of coffee and take them with them to the quarterdeck. The one night, as Jack passed through the mess hall on his way to the quarterdeck, there were several large trays of chocolate cake on the table. The area in the mess hall was dimly lighted with only a red light lighting the area. Jack proceeded to pick up several pieces of chocolate cake with chocolate icing, and headed for the quarterdeck. While walking toward the quarterdeck, Jack ate one piece of cake and carried the others. Upon arriving at the small office on the Quarterdeck, which was well lighted, Jack noticed that the icing on the cake was full of weevils. He had already eaten the one piece of cake, but he threw the rest of them overboard.

The crew of the Huntington was fortunate to have good cooks on the ship. The food was prepared properly and was always good to eat. This is not always true on Navy ships. In addition, because the Huntington was a new ship, there were no cockroaches or other vermin on the ship. One of Jack's favorites was the Wednesday morning breakfast. They served baked beans every Wednesday morning.

To get the meals, the crew members would stand in line at the appropriate time, pass by the servers, and sit down with a tray of food. Where the line existed, there were two rods, about two feet apart, on intervals, hanging from the overhead. At the bottom of these rods, there were small, very smooth hooks. Apparently this line of hooks was there to assist the cooking crew to move incoming food items into the galley. Anyway, when in the chow line, Jack liked to show off by putting his little fingers into the hooks, one into each of the hooks, and chin himself several times. He lifted his entire weight with his two little fingers. No one else could do it.

After several days, the ship left Genoa and, four and a half hours later, anchored in the Gulf of Spezia. They did not stay there very long, and got underway for Naples.

On the bridge while at sea, there was the Officer of the Deck, the Junior Officer of the Deck, helmsman, boatswains mate, messenger, quartermaster and possibly the bugler. On this one particular night, the Officer of the Deck was on the open bridge directly above the pilot house. The remainder of the people were in the pilot house. Somehow, with the conversation, it was determined that there should be a contest between the Junior Officer of the Deck, Ensign Davidson, and Jack McSherry, the Quartermaster. The proposed contest was to determine which one could do the most pushups. Ensign Davidson volunteered to go first. He laid on the deck of the pilot house, got into position and proceeded to do his pushups. As he did, everyone counted in unison the number of accomplished pushups. He rapidly did his pushups and, after doing 75 of them, he stood up in full confidence that he would be the winner. Then Jack got on the deck and began doing his pushups with the count going on by the cheerful audience. Jack stopped after doing 76 pushups and was the winner. Had Jack gone first, surely Ensign Davidson would have done one more than Jack.

Jack did not like to sleep in the confines of the living quarters. In port, he usually threw his mattress on the deck of the open bridge where he slept in the open air. However, when the ship was at sea, he could not sleep in the pilot house or the open bridge, so he would find other locations where he could throw his mattress on the deck and get a good night's sleep. At sea, he usually slept in some out of the way place on the signal bridge. This one evening, when the ship was cruising around in the Mediterranean, he chose to sleep in a narrow walkway outside and in front of the pilot house. This narrow walkway was intended for the officer of the deck to walk around for good visibility of the ocean ahead, however, they never used it for that purpose. In that space, Jack put his mattress down on the walkway and laid down for a good night's sleep. However, the wind was blowing rather hard and hitting Jack in the face. So he got up and found a large cardboard box. He slipped the end of the mattress into the box, then laid with his head in the box. He slept well. The next day, one of the other quartermasters told him that when the relieving officer of the deck saw someone sleeping there with his head in a cardboard box, he asked, "Who is that?" The quartermaster told him that it was McSherry. To this, the officer of the deck gave a familiar, Oh!

While cruising in the Mediterranean, on this one occasion Jack was in the pilot house as the quartermaster of the watch, the officer of the deck was on the open bridge above the pilot house. He called the pilot house over the voice tube and told Jack to determine the wind speed and direction. Jack looked out a porthole and observed the surface of the water. He noticed that waves were just forming, caused by the wind, and white caps were appearing on the waves. That happens when the wind reaches a velocity of 23 knots. Then he looked at the compass and compared the direction of the flow of the whitecaps and estimated the direction of the flow, and therefore, the direction of the wind. Comparing his observation with the compass, he determined that the flow was from bearing 234 degrees. He then called up the voice tube to the officer of the deck that the wind was coming from bearing 234 degrees at a velocity of 23 knots. This response was apparently sooner than the officer of the deck expected and he assumed that Jack did not calculate the wind velocity, and he told Jack to get the wind direction and the velocity and do it right. So Jack went through the proper procedure. He read the velocity of the wind and the wind direction on the anenometer, an instrument that determines these things. Then he proceeded to correct these determinations to allow for the speed of the ship. Upon completing his calculations, he called up to the officer of the deck and told him that the wind was coming from bearing 234 degrees at a velocity of 23 knots. This was the same figures that he had given him earlier. The officer of the deck had no comments other than a simple thank you.

On one of his liberties in Naples, Jack went into a small store which sold miscellaneous items. Jack found a soprano saxophone on one of the store shelves. Jack could play the alto saxophone, so he was interested in purchasing the soprano saxophone. The owner of the store, a friendly, middle-aged Italian offered to sell the saxophone to Jack for twenty dollars, American money, plus several bars of American perfumed soap. This was fine with Jack, so the next day he returned to the store with five bars of good-smelling soap. He gave the Owner a twenty dollar bill and the five bars of soap, and he purchased the saxophone. The Owner of the store was happy and pleased.

When he returned to the ship with the saxophone in its case, he concluded that it was not practical to put the saxophone in his locker, so he took it up to the pilot house where he unscrewed a steel plate from the deck of the pilot house and set it aside. He placed the saxophone, in its case, into the void area under the steel deck, then he screwed the steel deck plate back into its proper place. The saxophone remained stored there until the ship returned to the United States. Then he retrieved it and took it home. Recently Jack gave the saxophone to his fourteen year old grandson, Cody McSherry, who plays many instruments and is an extremely talented musician.

Italian Currency

During the month of October, 1946, the Huntington was in and out of Naples Harbor. They maneuvered in the Gulf of Salerno, and in the area southwest of the Isle of Capri.

On November 18, the ship got underway from Naples enroute to Alexandria, Egypt, arriving in Alexandria on the morning of November 23. Three days after arriving in Alexandria, Jack, on board a train, was heading south along the Nile River enroute to Cairo. After walking around the streets of Cairo for a while, Jack went into a factory where they made Fezs. He bought a fez in that factory.

This is a photo of the fez that Jack purchased in the factory in Cairo. Although shown here in a black & white photo, the fez is bright red.

Then he boarded a bus to go to the site of the Great Pyramids. The bus was very old and was traveling through desert areas on sandy roads. Along the way, they encountered a herd of water buffalo. Surprisingly, some of the water buffalo had little boys barely three or four years old, riding on the head of the water buffalos.

At the pyramids, Jack went into the great pyramid accompanied by two Arabs carrying torches for light. The inside of the pyramid was totally dark except for the torchlight. Shadows from the flickering torches were dancing on the walls inside the pyramid. They then went up a narrow, winding stairway to a passage above. From the passage above, there was a tunnel, about four feet wide and three feet high, where they crawled through on their hands and knees into the Pharaoh's tomb. The Pharaoh was not there. His body was spending eternity in a museum in Cairo.

The Great Pyramid and the Sphinx
1946

Upon exiting the pyramid, Jack mounted a camel and rode from the pyramids to the Sphinx. He rode the camel around the area of the sphinx to thoroughly observe the famous masterpiece, then he rode the return trip back to the Pyramids.

Interestingly, in the year 1985, Jack's son, Patrick was a student at Penn State University studying architecture. One evening he went to the auditorium to listen to a talk by Zahi Hawass, the person in charge of the care of all antiquities in Egypt. When Hawass concluded his lecture, he stated to the audience that they were all engineers and architects and he would like some advice pertaining to the Sphinx, and asked them to get in touch and talk to him. Mr.Hawass was temporarily in the United States and had an office at the University of Pennsylvania in Philadelphia. Patrick telephoned Hawass and made arrangements to meet him in his office. Jack, Patrick and another son, Jack III, who was a recent structural engineering graduate, drove to Philadelphia and met with Hawass. His problem was that the neck of the sphinx was carved through a layer of rock that was softer and had less strength, than the rest of the sphinx, and he was concerned that it may break off and allow the head to fall to the ground.

After listening to the details of the problem, and Jack having been at the sphinx in his Navy days, was familiar with the details of the sphinx, they reached a conclusion to solve the problem. They recommended to Hawass that he have a series of holes drilled through the top of the head and through the neck, and into the body of the sphinx. Then they advised him to insert large diameter reinforcing steel bars into the holes extending all the way from the top of the head and well into the body. These bars were to be sealed into the holes by filling the holes with a sand-cement grout.

The work as suggested was performed and the head and neck of the sphinx are securely held in place.

Jack riding a camel to the Sphinx, November 26, 1946

Jack rode the bus back to Cairo, and took the train from Cairo to Alexandria. He went back aboard the ship shortly after midnight that same day. When he walked up the gangplank to board the ship, Jack was wearing his fez rather than his official white hat. He dutifully saluted the Officer of the Deck as he stepped off the gangplank. The Officer of the Deck returned his salute with a smile.

While in Alexandria, the members of the crew were warned not to walk from the ship to the downtown area in groups of less than five so as not to be accosted by the natives and robbed, or preferably, take a taxi to the downtown area.

Not heeding this advice, Jack and a friend decided that they would walk downtown. As they walked through the suburban area of Alexandria where the houses were primarily shacks and all of the inhabitants were Arabs, Jack felt something hit his pantleg down near his shoes. He looked down and the pantleg was smeared with eggs. Before Jack could begin to gain his senses to determine what was happening, an old man, a balding little Arab, ran up to Jack and, with a cloth, he wiped the egg from Jack's pantleg. Jack was very appreciative of this kind old man and was preparing to thank him and give him some Egyptian piastres as a tip, when the man stood up and told Jack that he wanted a tip. That is when Jack was going to give him a little Egyptian money. However, the little old man said he did not want Egyptian money, he wanted American Money. At that point, the little old man held a knife against Jack just below his right side ribs and said that he wanted all of his money.

Jack concluded that he could land a quick punch into the face of the old man and send him flying, however, when he looked around, he and his friend were completely surrounded by a ring of mean looking Arabs. This called for a modification of his plans.

Just then, at the right moment, an Egyptian wearing a suit and a fez rode into the group of Arabs with his horse-drawn carriage and told the two Americans to climb aboard the carriage, which they did immediately. He then drove the two of them into the downtown area. However, before they could leave the carriage, he told them that he wanted to be paid. He wanted a large amount of money, at least three times the customary taxi fee. Jack was thankful to him for rescuing them, but thought that his request for payment was exorbitant. An Egyptian policeman was standing nearby and he heard the argument. His advice was for them was to pay the man what he was asking for. So Jack gave the carriage driver the money and left the carriage.

Looking back on the incident, Jack believes that the whole thing was an organized system for robbery and included, the old Arab, the circle of mean looking Arabs, the carriage driver, and the policeman.

Possibly Jack should have heeded the warning and instructions of the Navy and went down town in a taxi.

Egyptian coins

Egyptian Currency

Alexandria, Egypt
1946

On another liberty, Jack was walking, all alone, down a street in downtown Alexandria, a little after midnight heading for the ship, when a young boy, about six years old, approached him and wanted to sell him a blackjack. Jack declined and walked just a little faster toward the ship.

The Huntington left Alexandria on November 29, 1946, crossed the Mediterranean Sea, and anchored in the harbor at Taranto, Italy. This was a short visit and did not include any shore leave. The ship got underway the next morning and anchored in Paul's Bay, Malta. The next morning, the ship moved from Paul's Bay and moored to the dock in Valetta Harbor, Malta. That evening, Jack went ashore on liberty and walked around the streets of Malta. The next day, the ship left Malta and returned to Naples and tied up to the capsized Italian cruiser.

Ten days later, the Huntington left Naples. The next day she anchored at Villefranche, France. There wasn't much in Villefranche, so sometimes Jack walked the four miles to Nice, and sometimes he rode the bus.

After several days, they got underway from Villefranche and nine hours later moored to the dock at Marseille, France. The Huntington was at Marseille on News Years Eve, but Jack chose to stay on the ship. He figured that there would be too much commotion ashore.

French Currency

The Huntington left Marseille on January 5, 1947. Eighteen hours later she tied up to the dock in Genoa, Italy.

While on liberty in Genoa, Jack and two of his friends went to a movie in a theatre in downtown Genoa. It was a very big theatre, however, it was in the wintertime and there was no heat in the theatre. Even though they were wearing their peacoats they were cold, however, they watched the movie to the end. The movie starred Bob Hope and Bing Crosby. The Italian language was dubbed into the movie so Bing and Bob spoke Italian in the movie, however Bing sang in English.

After several days in Genoa, the Huntington moved on, cruising toward Malta. She anchored at Marsaxlokk, Malta. For several days, the ship maneuvered in the area around Malta, then returned to Naples.

After spending about two weeks in Naples, she again got underway enroute to Gibraltar where she moored to the dock.

After two days in Gibraltar, she again got underway and cruised into the Atlantic Ocean enroute to the West Indies to have a rendezvous at sea with the Naval Task Group 28.

As the ship was crossing the Atlantic, she entered into a heavy storm. The waves were about thirty feet high and the ship rolled as much as 39 degrees from vertical. Jack thought this was exciting and enjoyed every minute of it. The mess hall could not serve food during this time because of the extreme rolling of the ship, but they passed out sandwiches to the crew, and they hung coffee pots from the overhead (ceiling). The coffee was available to the crew as the pots swung back and forth. In going up or down a stairway, the person would be walking down a very steep slope, then suddenly the stairway would flatten out. Walking on a rolling ship is difficult, but fun.

During that storm, one night, Jack got out of his bunk at about 11:30 PM to go on Quartermaster watch on the bridge. He had to be on the bridge at 11:45, so he had a little time to spare. Even though it was February, and the ship was in a heavy storm, it was a balmy night, so Jack took a walk out onto the main deck just to watch the big dark waves. Suddenly, he heard a loud crash toward the bow of the ship. He knew that a wave broke across the bow and that the main deck would become flooded, so he ran toward the superstructure to open a hatch to get inside so that he would not get drenched with water. Before he got to the hatch, he was hit by a four-foot deep wave of water, which took him with it toward the side of the ship. As he was being swept overboard, he grabbed one of the cables of the railing on the side of the ship, held on, and pulled himself back onto the deck. He was now soaking wet, but it was time to go to the bridge for his Quartermaster watch. When he walked into the pilot house, someone said that he was soaking wet. He responded, "I am not!" That was the end of that.

After several days, the storm finally subsided.

About this time, while still cruising in the Atlantic, Jack was on Quartermaster watch in the pilot house when the officer of the deck, who was on the open bridge directly above the pilot house, called him through the voice tube to come up to the open bridge. Jack went up to the open bridge. The officer of the deck was a lieutenant junior Grade who came up through the ranks from an enlisted man. He was not a pleasant man, and apparently was out to prove something to Jack. He ordered Jack, in a very nasty tone of voice, to clean up the bulkhead of the open deck where someone threw up. Jack said that he would get someone immediately to clean it up. The officer responded in a nasty tone, "I told you to clean it up". Jack explained to him that he was on watch as the quartermaster of the watch and cannot leave his duties, and will get someone to clean it up. This only made the officer of the deck angrier, then he yelled at jack to get the church pennant down which was flying on the foremast of the ship. This pennant flies while church services are going on aboard the ship. Jack told the officer of the deck that church services are still in session, but when they are concluded in about ten minutes, he will take down the pennant because this is part of the quartermaster's duties. He yelled at jack to do as he was told. Jack took down the church pennant, but did not return to the bridge, instead he went down to the living quarters and laid in his bunk. The Officer of the deck put Jack on report for direct disobedience of orders of the officer of the deck.

Looking back on the incident, Jack was right in that it was improper for the officer of the deck to order him to do cleaning while he was on watch as the Quartermaster. However, Jack handled the situation very badly and incorrectly by refusing to do what was ordered. He should have performed the cleanup, then later reported the details of the incident to his Division Officer. His Division Officer would have filed a report of the incident with the Executive Officer. Without a doubt, the Officer of the deck would have been reprimanded for giving an improper order, and for improper conduct. Therefore Jack would have been exonerated of the charges.

After about a week, Jack was required to appear at Captain's Mast for a hearing concerning his disobedience of orders of the officer of the deck. This was a rather serious offense and Jack was not too sure what was going to happen to him. When he appeared at the hearing, the executive officer of the ship, Commander Gregor, was officiating in place of the Captain. Commander Gregor had been the navigator of the ship prior to being promoted to Executive Officer, so he knew Jack quite well since, as a quartermaster, Jack used to help him with the navigation. The officer of the deck proceeded to tell the Commander all about the episode on the bridge, making his case as well as he could. When he was finished, Commander Gregor asked Jack what he had to say in his defense. Jack responded that he had nothing to say. Commander Gregor then stated his verdict. He told Jack that when the ship gets back to the United States, he was scheduled to get a 20 day leave. His punishment was that the leave would be cancelled. Considering that Jack could have gotten brig time, or been demoted, Jack got off very easy. Jack believes that Commander Gregor stepped in to officiate at the hearing just to bail out a disastrous situation.

Six days after leaving Gibraltar, they joined Task Group 28. During those maneuvers, the Huntington was cruising along with many other ships of the fleet.

The Huntington had two pontoon planes on board. There was a hanger below the fantail where they were usually stored. However, out at sea they were mounted on catapults on the fantail. When these planes were to take off, they fired the catapult and the plane left the ship at a speed of sixty miles per hour. As they were cruising around with the fleet, Ensign Matthews took off in one of the planes on an observation flight. Jack was on watch in the pilot house at the time. The Captain and the Officer of the deck were also in the pilot house. The Officer of the deck was in contact with Matthews on the radio. Matthews was a cheerful man and a little on the wild side. Before entering the Navy, he was a bush pilot in Alaska. He enjoyed flying the Navy plane in an equally wild manner. On this particular day, as he was flying the plane around in the general area of the group of ships, and rather high in the air, he said on the radio that his engine stalled and he was having trouble restarting it. The Captain immediately took the radio and ordered Matthews to bail out. Matthews responded that he thinks he can start the engine in compression by diving it toward the ocean. As the Captain cussed, Matthews put the plane into a dive straight down toward the ocean. After diving at least halfway to the ocean, the engine started and Matthews pulled it out of the dive. The Captain cussed some more and said something about that crazy %$#&^%$. Matthews probably got an earful when he got back on board the ship and met with the Captain.

While maneuvering with that same task force, Jack was steering the ship, when the officer of the deck gave him orders to follow in the wake of the ship in front of them. This was an unusual command, because customarily the helmsman steers by compass, or by direct orders from the officer of the deck for each turn that is made. The task force was doing a lot of turning and zig-zagging at the time.

Jack followed in the wake of the ship which they were following. Each time that ship turned, Jack turned in the same location following the wake of the ship ahead. It was like driving a car on a road.

During those maneuvers, the Huntington was cruising single file with several other cruisers to get some anti-aircraft gunnery practice. The targets for the practice were unmanned drones. The ship directly in front of the Huntington was the USS Juneau, an anti-aircraft cruiser. The Juneau began shooting at the drones as the Huntington crew watched. They were exploding close to the drones but never hit any of them.

Next it was the Huntington's turn. As the drone flew over, the first shot from one of the Huntington's 40 Millimeter anti-aircraft guns brought the drone down.

Jack bragged about that incident for years. The specialty cruiser did not shoot any of the drones down, but the Huntington shot one down on her first shot. About forty years after that incident, Jack went to a reunion of the Huntington. There he met one of the bakers from the ship. Although he was a baker, his duty during general quarters was to man one of the 40 millimeter guns. He told his listeners that he shot down the drone, but got into trouble for doing so. His

85

orders were to shoot close to the drone, but do not hit it. Jack never knew that, but he quit bragging about the ship's great shooting ability.

After maneuvering with the Task Force for about two weeks, the Huntington anchored In Guantanamo Bay, Cuba.

For the next two weeks, the Huntington maneuvered in the area of Culebra Island and had gunnery practice.

On March14, the ship left the West Indies and cruised to the Brooklyn Navy Yard where they entered three days later and moored to the dock.

When the ship arrived in the Brooklyn Navy yard, most of the crew went home on leave. Jack, of course, did not get a leave. Interestingly enough, when the plan of the day was posted, as usual it listed all of the officers of each department that would be on duty that day as the head of the department. Along with lieutenants, ensigns, commanders and other officers of the various departments, Jack, as a Quartermaster 3rd class was listed as the head of the navigation department. He was the senior person of the navigation department on board the ship at that time.

Being the senior person, of the Navigation Division, on board the ship, Jack gave himself a 72 hour liberty each weekend. Even though his leave was cancelled, Jack went home anyway.

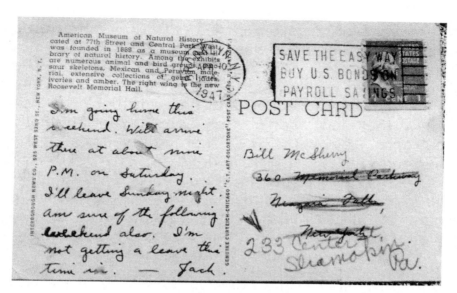

On this card, Jack is telling his brother that he will not be getting a leave this time while back in the United States. He did not tell him why.

The ship was moored to the dock in the Brooklyn Navy Yard from March 18 to April 28. During that time, Jack went on liberty into New York City on a regular basis where he went to the top of the Empire State Building, and to several live radio broadcasting shows. He also went to movie theatres where, between showings of the movie, famous musicians would appear on stage for a concert. Jack saw, among others, Cab Callaway and Buddy Rich. Each weekend, he travelled home to Tharptown on liberty.

One time, while in the Brooklyn Navy yard, Jack and one of his friends went on liberty into New York City, as they quite often did. This time, around midnight, they were walking down the street toward the Navy

Yard when they walked past a bar. The doors of the bar were open and it was all lit up. They looked into the bar and saw many of their shipmates inside. The two of them walked into the bar. With this, all of the shipmates were hooting and hollering because they knew that Jack didn't drink and did not normally patronize the bars. They were all yelling to the bartender to give Jack a drink on them. So Jack walked up to the bar and ordered a glass of milk. Everyone screamed and the bartender gave Jack a glass of milk. When he drank it, they yelled to give him another. Jack then drank a second glass of milk, thanked everyone, and left the bar.

During the stay in the Brooklyn Navy yard, there was only a skeleton crew on board the ship. There was one other quartermaster on board besides Jack. One day in the chart house, they opened the lid to the box containing the ship's chronometers and found that all of the chronometers were stopped. Each one of the quartermasters thought that the other was winding them. Allowing the chronometers to stop is a court martial offense, so they immediately determined that they were going to restart them. A log was kept for each chronometer. The amount of error from the correct time was recorded daily in the log for each chronometer. The errors being different, each chronometer had a slightly different time. To start the chronometers at precisely the correct time, they had to listen to the time signal from Washington, DC, on the radio. The other quartermaster listened to the time signal and Jack prepared to start the chronometer which was to be started first. When the exact time came, he yelled "mark", and Jack started winding the chronometer. The first one started right up and was on the correct time to match the error recorded in the log book. They did the same thing with the second chronometer and it started, but several seconds later than the error recorded in the log book. Then they went to the third chronometer. When he yelled "Mark", Jack started winding the chronometer, but it did not start, so he shook it, and banged on it. Finally it started but about 20 seconds later than it should have. To allow for the late start of the two chronometers, Jack had to modify the recordings in the log book. It was easy to change the recordings slightly to allow for the few seconds on the one chronometer, but for the twenty seconds , it was a greater deal. Jack erased the error listings in the log book for about a month prior to the restart. He then divided the twenty seconds equally among the 30 days and recorded these new errors. The result was that all three chronometers were running and their errors conformed to the errors as listed in the log book.

On April 28, 1947, the ship got underway from the Brooklyn Navy Yard and anchored in Gravesend Bay to load ammunition.

The next day, the ship left Gravesend Bay enroute to the Naval Base at Newport, Rhode Island and anchored in the Narragansett Bay. From May 7 to May 12, the ship participated in maneuvers in the area around Narragansett Bay.

Jack, aboard the USS Huntington, May 10, 1947

On May 12, the ship went to Norfolk, Virginia, arriving there the next morning. Later that same day, she left Norfolk and arrived in Newport the next evening.

On May 20, 1947, the Huntington left Newport enroute to Gibraltar. The first four days of the crossing of the ocean, the sea was calm, but visibility was very bad because of a thick fog. On the fifth day, the sea got rougher along with haze and rain.

The Rock of Gibraltar From five miles away on a foggy day.
May 30, 1947

When at sea it was customary to have a seaman from the deck force come to the pilot house to steer the ship. All they had to do was to turn the wheel as necessary to hold the rudder in the right position to steer the required course as shown on the compass. These sailors had no steering experience the first time they came to the bridge, so the Quartermaster of the watch had to show them how to do it.

On the way to Gibraltar, a seaman from the deck force, William Scharninghausen, arrived in the pilot house to steer the ship. He questioned why he was sent up to steer the ship because not only couldn't he steer a ship, he couldn't even drive a car. Jack showed him how to handle the ship's wheel and how to read the compass. All he had to do was to steer the ship on whatever course the officer of the deck commanded. After several trips to the pilot house, he became a fairly competent helmsman. On one occasion when he was on the helm, he received a command through the voice tube from the officer of the deck who was on the open bridge above the pilot house. The officer of the deck said that the Captain is at the movies on the fantail of the ship, and he wanted the helmsman to make a sharp turn to port (to the left), but he wanted him to make the turn very slowly and gradually so as not to rock the ship in any manner. Receiving this command, Scharninghausen looked at Jack with his mouth hanging open. Jack asked him if he wanted him to take over and make the turn. He happily stepped aside and allowed Jack to take the wheel. Jack turned the ship very slowly and gently so that no one on the ship could feel that the ship was turning. When Jack completed the turn, he gave the wheel back to Scharninghausen. As soon as Scharninghausen was back on the wheel, the officer of the deck called down through the voice tube and said, "Helmsman, that was very well done". Sharninghausen responded, "thank you sir". He took all of the credit for the good turn.

The quartermasters and other people on the bridge got to know Scharninghausen quite well after he steered the ship several times. Jack learned that Scharninghausen played the cornet, and another bugler was needed on the bridge. So they arranged for Scharninghausen to be transferred from the deck force to the Navigation Division. It worked out well. Scharninghausen became a bugler and, as of this day, is still a close friend of Jack's.

It happened that Scharninghausen's bunk was at the bottom of the three tier bunks, and Jack's bunk was at the top of the same tier. One day, they were horsing around. No one was in the center bunk. Somehow, Jack accidentally unhooked the center bunk and it fell down and hit Scharninghausen on the lip creating a large cut on his lip.

The next day, as the ship was entering port, Scharninghausen was concerned that he probably would not be able to play the 20 second blast on the bugle over the public address system at the precise time that the anchor was dropped, as is the tradition. So Jack took the bugle and played a 40 second blast when the anchor dropped. While Scharninghausen's lip was sore, Jack played quite a few bugle calls for him, as necessary. On May 30, the ship anchored in Gibraltar bay.

Jack and Scharninghausen went on liberty into the town of Gibraltar and into the town's Alameda Park.

A gentleman relaxing in Alameda Park on the
Rock of Gibraltar, June 1, 1947

The next day, before going ashore to Gibraltar on liberty, Jack was looking at the Rock through the ship's very powerful, tripod mounted binoculars. He saw many caves that were carved into the sides of the rock, each containing a big gun. But on top of the Rock was a very large gun aimed toward the Strait of Gibraltar. He went ashore on liberty and walked through the town of Gibraltar which was at the base of the Rock. He followed a path up a hill which went through Alameda Park, and which contained many flowers and benches. He continued walking up the hill because he wanted to get a good look at that monstrous gun on the top of the Rock. When he got within several hundred feet of the gun, he was confronted by a British soldier with a rifle. The soldier told Jack that he could go no further. Looking at the soldier and the gun, Jack turned around and went back down the hill.

On June 5, The Huntington got underway from Gibraltar. Operated at sea in the vicinity of the Northwest coast of Africa.

The next day, anchored at Tangier, a free city located within the country of Morocco. Jack went on liberty and walked around in Tangier all afternoon and evening. The next day because of very high winds in the harbor at Tangier, some merchant ships were dragging their anchors and were struggling to fight the winds and leave the harbor so as not to be washed up on the rocks. The Huntington raised anchor and went out to sea to ride out the storm as a precaution against dragging anchor during the night.

On June 7th the wind was too strong to anchor the ship, so she cruised around in the close proximity of Gibraltar. However, the following day, the ship went back into Tangier and anchored. A short time later, the wind picked up again, so as a precaution, the Huntington raised anchor and moved to the outer bay and again anchored. Being anchored in the outer bay and with the very rough waters, there was no liberty for the crew because the liberty boats could not operate under those conditions.

Tangier, June 6, 1947

The following day, even though the ship was anchored in the outer bay, the winds and rough water calmed down somewhat so that the liberty boats could make their runs to the mainland. So Jack once again went ashore and into the City of Tangier. He hiked around the streets of tangier. An Arab approached him and offered to sell him a knife. It was one of those curved ones that the Arabs wear under their robes. Jack bought the knife and concealed it under his jumper to take back to the ship.

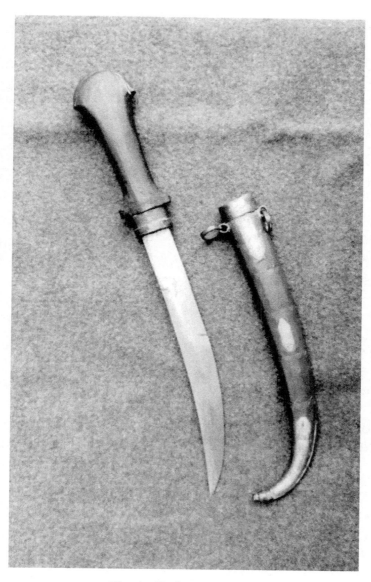

The knife from Tangier
June 6, 1947

Morrocan Currency

When it was time to go back to the ship, Jack walked to the dock to take the liberty boat to the ship. However, when he got to the dock, the Admiral and his staff were aboard the Admiral's barge preparing to leave for the ship. The Admiral recognized Jack and invited him to ride to the ship with him in the barge. Jack was honored to accept the ride.

Jack painting the superstructure of the Huntington
June 12, 1947

Periodically, the Executive Officer would order the ship to be repainted. The color of the paint was labeled haze gray. When this command occurred, all enlisted men on the ship were expected to participate. Jack never objected to this. He always repainted the exterior of the pilot house and the chart house.

On one occasion, Jack decided that the metal guard behind the front running light on the foremast of the ship needed painting. This guard was placed behind the light to ensure that the light could only be seen from the front of the ship and to certain angles to the left and to the right of the light. To get to the running light, he had to climb a ladder consisting of metal rungs attached to the mast. He climbed up that mast, carrying his can of paint and a paint brush, and painted the metal guard. The light was about 120 feet above the water line.

On June 13, the ship raised anchor and headed for Oran, Algeria, arriving there the next morning. Jack and his friend Bill Scharninghausen went on liberty into the city of Oran.

Mosque, Joan of Arc
Oran, Algeria

The following day, Jack was assigned to go ashore into Oran on Shore Patrol. The shore patrol serves as police for the Navy to handle any disturbances involving American navy personnel on shore, and to assist in keeping the sailors from creating situations that would be offensive toward the host country.

This photo shows Jack standing on the open bridge of the Huntington, wearing the proper gear to go ashore on shore patrol duty in Oran, Algeria.

Notice on the photograph, just to the left of Jack's right arm, is the Captain's chair, which is reserved only for the Captain. Notice the can-shaped item hanging on the side of the chair. A new captain had just recently taken command of the Huntington. At sea, Jack noticed that when the captain sat in that chair, he would light up a cigarette. Upon finishing the cigarette, he would throw the cigarette butt on the deck. Jack did not appreciate that, because the Bridge was his hangout and also his responsibility to keep it clean. Jack took a can-shaped ash tray from the bulkhead in the chart house. He attached a double wire hook to the can with some fancy ropework and painted the ropework white. When the captain was not on the bridge, Jack took his fancy ashcan and hung it on the side of the Captain's chair.

The next time the captain was sitting in his chair, Jack was above on the signal bridge watching. Before long, the captain lit up a cigarette, and when finished, he crushed the cigarette out on the new ashcan and dropped the butt into it. Jack was pleased.

Jack went ashore at eight o'clock in the morning, wearing his Shore Patrol identification badge and armed with a large wooden club. While on patrol of the streets of Oran, Jack teamed up with a French sailor who was also on shore patrol duty for his country. They walked around the town together, but could not talk to each other because they did not know each other's language.

At noon, the Frenchman left Jack to go to some location where he would be relieved of his watch, so now Jack was walking around by himself. Jack got to thinking, how is he going to be relieved and where. Anyway, Jack never did get relieved, so he walked around the city of Oran until midnight. Then he rode the liberty boat back to the ship. It was a long day, but he enjoyed every minute of it.

For the next several days, Bill Scharninghausen and Jack walked around the streets of Oran. It was a different and interesting place.

France Manca, Jack, and Claudie Manca
Oran, Algeria, June 16, 1947

The girls pictured above were French girls who lived in Oran. The girl named France made Jack's acquaintance the day before while Jack was on shore patrol duty. The girls are sisters and they invited Jack to go to their home to meet their parents. Jack invited Scharninghausen to go along. In going to the Manca home, they walked through the Arab area, the Spanish area and then arrived in the French area. Some natives gave them snarling looks as they walked by.

They spent several hours visiting the Manca family. They were very nice people and spoke some English, so all went well. Mrs. Manca poured a jigger of cognac for each Scharninghausen and Jack. Jack would have preferred not to drink the cognac, but he drank it with a smile and happiness. They had a nice visit with a nice family.

They left the Manca home close to midnight, went outside and starting walking along on the sidewalk. They observed that there were many little walkways and alleys leading off of the sidewalk. The alleys were dark and the street was dimly lit. Scharninghausen and Jack then decided to walk in the middle of the street so that no one could reach out of the alley and pull them into the darkness.

They walked the entire way back to the dock in the middle of the street and got back to the ship safely.

On the 18th of June, the Huntington left Oran and the next day anchored in Chenova Bay

Jack on the beach at Chenova Bay
June 19, 1947

Several days later, along with the USS Houston and the USS Fargo, The Huntington left Chenova Bay for gunnery practice around Malta. This practice continued for about a week.

The Huntington's 40mm anti-aircraft guns in action
During gunnery practice.
June 25, 1947

The Huntington took off for Rapallo Bay, Italy. The ship stayed in Rapallo for about a week. Jack went on liberty where he went boating (in a rowboat) and swimming and watched a Madonna celebration.

Jack boating in Rapallo Bay
July 5, 1947

The ship got underway from Rapallo on the morning of July 7, and moored to the dock in Genoa three hours later. That evening Jack went on liberty in Genoa. After spending almost two weeks in Genoa, the ship left that city and anchored in the Gulf of Salerno. The next three days the ship had gunnery practice at sea.

On July 21, The Huntington left the Gulf of Salerno enroute to Villefranche, France. As they were cruising along in the Mediterranean sea, Jack was standing quartermaster watch in the pilot house. He looked out a porthole on the starboard side of the ship and saw a whale swimming along on the surface of the water.

After watching the whale for a short period of time, he realized that the ship and the whale were on a collision course. The officer of the deck was, at the time, on the open bridge directly above the pilot house. Jack figured that the officer of the deck was watching the whale and would adjust the ship's course or speed at the appropriate time so as not to have a collision. Soon, it became apparent to Jack that the whale and the ship were about to collide. Apparently the officer of the deck did not see the whale. Jack, without the authority to do so, moved the engine order telegraphs to reverse both engines to full speed reverse, and at the same time turned the ship's wheel to a 90 degree turn to port.

This was a drastic change in speed and direction. The ship shook and quivered violently. When all settled, there was no collision, the ship did not hit the whale. The ship was not damaged and the whale was not killed or injured. The strange thing about this whole event was that, although the whole incident was very obvious throughout the ship, there was never any mention of the incident. Jack was not chastised nor was he complemented. Possibly the officer of the deck took all of the blame or the credit, and was thereby excused for all of the commotion.

The ship anchored in Villefranche Bay on July 22. Most days while anchored in Villefanche, Jack and Scharninghausen went on liberty to Nice either by bus or walked the four miles. Also while in Villefranche, Jack and Scharninghausen went on liberty to Monte Carlo.

USS Huntington anchored in Villefranche Bay
July 23, 1947

The Direction of the

Monaco

have the pleasure in inviting the

NAVAL FORCES

during these stay in Tangier to the

THE DANSANT

daily from 5 p. m. to 7 p. m.

---

20 FAMOUS SPANISH ARTISTS, 20

=== A N D ===

TWO WELL KNOWN SPANISH ORCHESTRA

"Editorial Tánger"

The ship left Villefranche and the next day moored to the dock in Maddalena, Sardinia. Went on liberty in Maddalena. After about a week in Maddalena, the ship got underway and the next day moored to a dock in Pozzioli, Italy to refuel the ship. Then, the day after that, got underway again and anchored in the Gulf of Naples. On August 11 got underway from the Gulf of Naples for operations with other ships in the area around the Gulf of Salerno. While involved in those operations, The Huntington answered an emergency call from the merchant ship, John Prinz of Sardinia, met the ship and gave medical aid. That evening, the Huntington anchored in the Gulf of Salerno. Several days later, the ship returned to Naples bay.

The Ruins of Pompeii, August 17, 1947

The amphitheater at the ruins of Pompeii,
August 17, 1947

The admission ticket to the ruins of Pompeii

A commercial advertisement - Pompeii

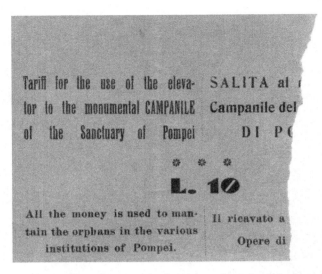

The stub of a ticket for a ride in the cathedral's elevator into the bell tower

On August 18, 1947, the ship got underway for Trieste, arriving there two days later. Spending the next ten days moored to the dock in Trieste, Jack and Scharninghausen went into the downtown area regularly on liberty.

A commercial for a Trieste Theater

Rear Admiral Burroughs, August 31, 1947

August 31, left Trieste and on September 5, 1947, moored to the dock at Gibraltar. While the ship was moored at Gibraltar, she was refueled. On the afternoon of September 5th, the Huntington got underway from Gibraltar.

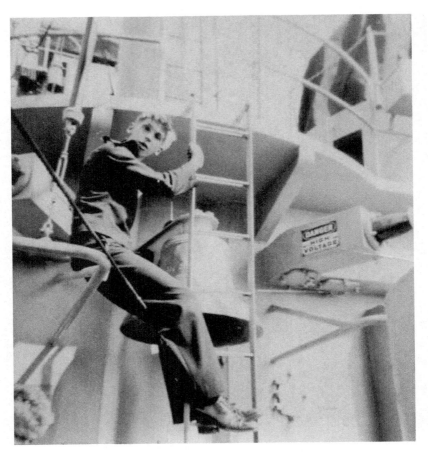

Bill Scharninghausen polishing the ship's bell
September 11, 1947

On the 13th of September, 1947, she moored to a buoy in Narraganset bay at Newport Rhode Island. From this date through October 9, the ship was in and out of the harbor on practice runs.

Emily Anderson and Jack Visiting Aunt
Ruth & Uncle Bertlette Burrell Bear Gap,
PA, September 28, 1947 Jack was on a
10-day leave from the navy

For the entire time that Jack was on the USS Huntington, he carried a small notebook in which he recorded every course and distance that the ship traveled. When he was discharged from the Navy, he put this notebook with his memoirs.

In 1994, the members of the crew of the Huntington held a ship's reunion in Huntington, West Virginia, the City for which the ship was named. In preparation for this reunion, Jack pulled his artifacts and memoirs together to take to the reunion. He decided to try to plot the courses and distances on charts so that he could take that with him to the reunion. Surprisingly to Jack, all of the recorded courses and distances plotted perfectly on the charts to the correct destinations.

Jack plotted these courses on two charts. One of the charts showed all the courses in the Atlantic Ocean, and the other showed all of the courses in the Mediterranean.

In addition, he made listings of each individual journey from port to port, assigning them a number. This number was put on the chart to identify that particular leg of travel. The names of the port which the ship was leaving and the port being entered were listed, showing the date of departure and the date of arrival. It also listed the distance travelled between those ports. Many of the individual journeys were duplicated in location.

It was Jack's suggestion to hold the ship's 50th anniversary reunion in her namesake town, Huntington, West Virginia. Everyone agreed, so that's where they went. However, the people of Huntington and the City Government had no interest whatsoever and totally ignored the crew of the ship. The only people there who talked to the crew was the Navy Recruiters, and members of the Huntington crew visited them daily.

The charts and listing of port data follows:

Courses and distances traveled by the USS Huntington in the Atlantic Ocean.

February 23, 1946 –October 19, 1947

ATLANTIC OCEAN

1.	Philadelphia to Norfolk	3/27 – 3/29, 1946	174 Miles
2.	Norfolk to Guantanamo	4/1 – 4/4, 1946	952
3.	Guantanamo to San Juan	5/3 – 5/19, 1946	712
4.	San Juan to Guantanamo	5/22 – 5/24, 1946	615
5.	Guantanamo to Philadelphia	6/28 – 7/1, 1946	1104
6.	Philadelphia to Naples	7/23 – 8/5, 1946	4299
7.	Gibraltar to Guantanamo	2/8 – 3/1, 1947	3735
8.	Guantanamo to New York	3/7 – 3/18, 1947	2208
9.	New York to Newport	4/29 – 4/30, 1947	139
10.	Newport to Norfolk	5/12 – 5/13, 1947	376
11.	Norfolk to Newport	5/13 – 5/14, 1947	376
12.	Newport to Gibraltar	5/20 – 5/30, 1947	3168
13.	Gibraltar to Newport	9/5 – 9/13, 1947	3168
		Total Miles	19900

© Jack L. McSherry, Jr.   1994

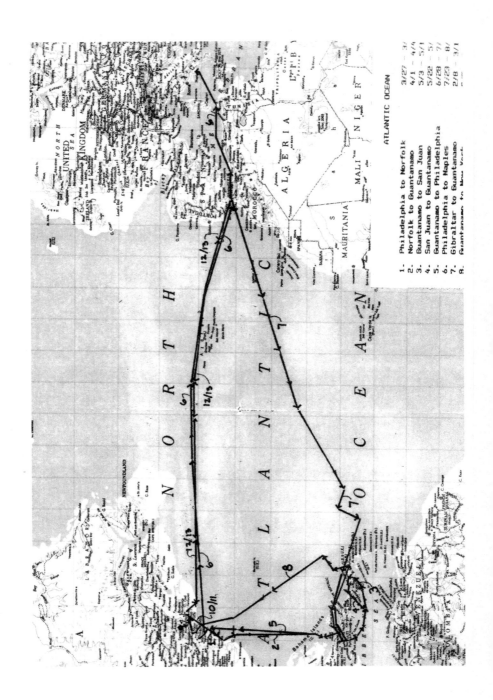

ATLANTIC OCEAN

1. Philadelphia to Norfolk   3/27 - 3/
2. Norfolk to Guantanamo   4/1 - 4/4
3. Guantanamo to San Juan   5/3 - 5/
4. San Juan to Guantanamo   5/22 - 5/
5. Guantanamo to Philadelphia   6/28 - 7/
6. Philadelphia to Naples   7/23 - 8/
7. Gibraltar to Guantanamo   2/8 - 3/1
8. Guantanamo to New York   --

MEDITERRANEAN SEA

#	Route	Date	Miles
1.	Naples to Trieste	8/6 – 8/8, 1946	875 Miles
2.	Trieste to Venice	8/20, 1946	83
3.	Venice to Trieste	8/26, 1946	83
4.	Trieste to Naples	9/11 – 9/14, 1946	875
5.	Naples to Malta	9/23 – 9/24, 1946	323
6.	Malta to Naples	9/26 – 9/27, 1946	323
7.	Naples to Leghorn	9/27 – 9/28, 1946	345
8.	Leghorn to Genoa	10/3, 1946	106
9.	Genoa to La Spezia	10/8, 1946	51
10.	La Spezia to Naples	10/10 – 10/11, 1946	389
11.	Naples to Alexandria	11/18 – 11/23, 1946	1128
12.	Alexandria to Taranto	11/29 – 12/3, 1946	1212
13.	Taranto to Malta	12/4 – 12/6, 1946	327
14.	Malta to Naples	12/9 – 12/10, 1946	347
15.	Naples to Villefranche	12/19 – 12/20, 1946	400
16.	Villefranche to Marseilles	12/27, 1946	134
17.	Marseilles to Genoa	1/5 – 1/6, 1947	317
18.	Genoa to Malta	1/11 – 1/13, 1947	608
19.	Malta to Naples	1/16 – 1/17, 1947	323
20.	Naples to Gibraltar	2/3 – 2/6, 1947	1014
21.	Gibraltar to Tangier	6/5 – 6/6, 1947	39
22.	Tangier to Oran	6/13 – 6/14, 1947	257
23.	Oran to Chenova Bay	6/18 – 6/19, 1947	172
24.	Chenova Bay to Malta	6/21 – 6/23, 1947	613
25.	Malta to Rapallo	6/27 – 6/30, 1947	593
26.	Rapallo to Genoa	7/7, 1947	19
27.	Genoa to Gulf of Salerno	7/14 – 7/15, 1947	373
28.	Gulf of Salerno to Villefranche	7/21 – 7/22, 1947	396
29.	Villefranche to Maddelena	8/1 – 8/2, 1947	179
30.	Maddelena to Naples	8/7 – 8/9, 1947	242
31.	Naples to Trieste	8/18 – 8/20, 1947	842
32.	Trieste to Gibraltar	8/31 – 9/5, 1947	1511

Total Miles   14499

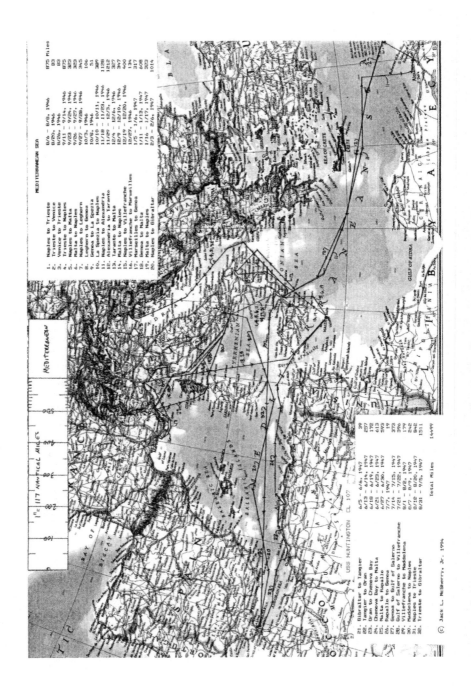

CHAPTER V

TRANSFERRED FROM THE USS HUNTINGTON
TO DESTROYER MINE SWEEPERS.

On October 10, 1947, Jack was transferred from the USS Huntington to the Destroyer Mine Sweeper, USS Jeffers DMS 27. Went aboard the USS Jeffers in Boston, Massachusetts on October 13.

On October 18, the Jeffers got underway from Boston, went through the Cape Cod Canal, and moored to a buoy in the Narraganset Bay.

On October 19, Jack was transferred from the USS Jeffers to the USS Ellyson DMS 19.

Jack was not particularly happy about being transferred from the Huntington to the Destroyers, however, that's the way it works in the Navy. The Huntington was a new ship and was clean, and unlike most ships, it had no cockroaches or other vermin aboard. The food on the Huntington was excellent. Jack is now on board the USS Ellyson, a destroyer that saw considerable action in World War II. The Ellyson is now classified as a destroyer mine sweeper, and the present duty of that ship is to pull targets through the water for the cruisers and battleships to practice their gunnery. Fortunately, the Ellyson discontinued pulling targets about the time that Jack went aboard. For the first three days that Jack was aboard, the Ellyson was maneuvering around the area of Narraganset Bay. The Ellyson had on board many cockroaches. They could be seen regularly in the mess hall and the heads (restrooms). Jack had one unfortunate incident shortly after he got on the ship. He was in the mess hall eating his soup when his spoon picked up a cockroach which drowned in his soup. Jack ate carefully after that.

On October 24, the Ellyson got underway for New York City and entered the Hudson River enroute to Kingston, New York on a goodwill tour. It happened that the only other Quartermaster on the ship was a first class Quartermaster. Jack was still rated as third class quartermaster. Whenever a ship proceeds to go up a river, or in and out of port, or any other special type of cruising, a Quartermaster is required to steer the ship. However, when the ship was preparing to leave New York Harbor and go into the Hudson River, the first class quartermaster was lying in his bunk with a hangover. Apparently this was his regular routine. So, Jack, being the only other quartermaster on the ship, told the first class quartermaster to remain in his bunk. Jack told him that he will do all of the steering of the ship up the river.

Customarily, one person steers the ship for four hours, then he is relieved by another person. For this cruise up the Hudson River, Jack steered the ship for the entire seven hour trip. This was no problem, he enjoyed every minute of it. However, since the Officers of the Deck, and all of the other personnel on the bridge, are relieved every four hours, no one knew that Jack was on the wheel for seven hours. Had they known, it would have meant trouble for the first class quartermaster, who was in his bunk for the entire trip.

Cruising up the river was different than cruising at sea. The channel was narrower, and there were interesting things to see on the shore along the way. The ship passed Sing Sing Penitentiary on the starboard side, and, later, passed West Point Military Academy on the port side. They also passed under many bridges along the way.

Upon arriving at Kingston, New York, the water in the river was getting much shallower, to the point that the ship's screws (propellers) were occasionally hitting the bottom of the river. However, they managed to maneuver the ship alongside the dock and moored to the dock.

Kingston was celebrating an anniversary of the city. The people of the City were very receptive of the crew of the ship, and were very friendly. The ship stayed at Kingston for three days. On Saturday evening, the people honored the crew at a big dance and dinner in a local ballroom.

On October 28, 1947, the ship left Kingston and returned to Newport, Rhode Island where they moored to a buoy in the Narragansett Bay.

During the following month, the Ellyson maneuvered in the area around Narragansett Bay, returning to port regularly during that time. As this was occurring, and while the ship was in port, Jack went on liberty to Fall River, Massachusetts, and on Liberty to home on the weekends.

As usual, when on liberty at home, on Sunday evening it was time to travel back to the ship. The procedure was to walk to Shamokin and get on the "Lakes to

Sea" bus which went to New York City. In New York, Jack would get on a train which took him to Providence, Rhode Island. He then boarded a bus from Providence which took him to the Newport naval Station. At the Naval station, he waited on the dock for a liberty boat to come in to take him to the ship which was moored to a buoy in Narragansett Bay.

On the one return trip, during that time period, as usual Jack was sleeping in his seat on the bus. He knew that he would be alright sleeping because New York City was the last stop for the bus, and that is where he would get off. However, on this trip, the person sitting alongside Jack on the bus woke Jack and said we're in Newark, is this where you want to get off. Being half asleep, Jack thought he said New York, and he got off the bus. When he got off the bus, everything was pitch dark, including the station, and the bus was driving away. So there stands Jack, holding his overnight bag in Newark, New Jersey. He did manage to find a taxi. The taxi driver agreed to drive Jack to the railroad station in New York City for $ 15.00. Since Jack's pay in the Navy was $ 50.00 per month, that was an exorbitant amount of money. He had no choice, he took the taxi to New York. In New York, he was too late to take the train that he usually rode and took the next train following the same route to Providence. He finally arrived at the boat dock in the Newport Naval Station, arriving there at about 8:30 in the morning. The last liberty boat to the ship was scheduled to leave the dock at 7:30. However, the last liberty boat did not leave the dock on schedule because of stormy and rough water in the bay, leaving several sailors stranded on the dock. So the master at Arms handling the operations at the dock told Jack that he will say that Jack was there on time for the last boat, along with the other sailors and was not late. At about that time, Jack watched his ship heading out to sea without him.

The Ellyson was out at sea for several days. In the meantime, Jack had a bunk at the Naval Station and ate his meals in the mess hall. When the ship returned to port, Jack went back to the ship, and all was well.

On November 29, the Ellyson left Narraganset Bay enroute to Charleston, South Carolina. On December 1, the ship moored to the dock in Charleston.

CHAPTER VI

TO PANAMA AND THE USS ORION AS-18

On December 12, 1947 Jack was transferred from the Ellyson with orders to report to the Philadelphia Naval Receiving Station on January 5th. That gave him a 24 day leave to spend at home.

After spending his leave at home, Jack reported to the Naval Receiving Station in Philadelphia on January 5, 1948. The next day, he left Philadelphia by train and went to Baltimore. He boarded a commercial passenger steamer and left Baltimore at 6:00 PM, January 6 and arrived in Norfolk, Virginia at 6:00 AM the next morning.

On January 8 1948, he went aboard the USS President Adams, a Navy Transport Ship, as a passenger for passage to Balboa, Canal Zone, in Panama. The next day, the ship got underway and three days later moored to the dock in Guantanamo bay.

On January 14, got underway from Guantanamo and moored to the dock in Chaguaramas Bay, Trinidad. That evening Jack and Bob Filkins went on liberty to the town of Port of Spain in Trinidad. While in Port of Spain, Jack and Filkins took a walk into the countryside. They came to an area where a trail led into a woods alongside the road. With curiosity, they followed the trail into the woods, and as a precaution, kept a watchful eye up into the trees as they walked so as to spot any python snakes that may be hanging in the trees. They walked a little farther into the woods where they decided to turn around and go back to the road. As they were emerging from the woods, they stood there for a while and studied the landscape. As they stood there, a native of the area was walking by. When he saw the two American sailors, he cautioned them not to go into the woods. He said there were some mean wild boar living in there and last week someone walked up that trail and was never seen again. Jack and Filkins looked at each other, thanked the man, and walked back to the public road.

On January 20, The USS President Adams got underway from Trinidad and headed south. The north coast of South America was visible most of the next day. Three days of cruising south and the ship moored to the dock in Coco Solo, Canal Zone. They then went to Colon, Panama, got aboard a train pulled with an old steam engine, and rode through the jungles of Panama, arriving in Balboa, Canal Zone after a trip of 1 ½ hours.

On January 23, 1948, upon arrival in Balboa, the Navy personnel took formation on a dock in the Rodman Naval Station. It was there that Jack received the information that he was assigned to the crew of the USS Orion AS 18, a submarine tender. The Orion was tied up to that dock, so Jack went aboard.

The Orion was a very large ship, weighing about 25000 tons. On board, she had machine shops, a foundry, carpenter shop, and all other shops as necessary to make any part for a submarine that may
be required. The ship also contained many cockroaches. Alongside the Orion there were eight submarines moored to the dock. The Orion was the caretaker for those submarines.

USS Orion AS18

On board the Orion, Jack met the other quartermasters and was assigned to his bunk. He was now a crew member of the Orion.

On January 27, 1948 the USS Orion got underway for maneuvers in the vicinity of Cocos Island, an uninhabited Island in the Pacific Ocean. After the day's operations, they anchored in Chatham Bay, Cocos Island. The next day, the ship got underway and approached Valladolid Rock where they fired their guns at the rock, for practice, for about an hour, then they returned to the Rodman Naval base in Balboa, Canal Zone, where they moored to the dock.

Jack
Panama City, Panama
Feb. 3, 1948

On February 1, Jack went on liberty, for the first time, to Panama City, Panama. As was his custom, Jack roamed the streets of Panama City to get to know the city. Downtown Panama City was a modern city with churches, stores and other commercial buildings, plus traffic on the streets. Going toward the suburban area, there was a rather slummy neighborhood, then passing through that area and going further out of the City there were fancy estates where the wealthy people of Panama resided. Beyond that was farm land.

Electricians Mate Bob Filkins at the switchboard for the forward engine room of the USS Orion February 3, 1948

133

On February 19, 1948 the USS Orion got underway from the Rodman Naval Station, and proceeded into the Panama Canal, and continued through the canal's locks, and through the entire length of the Canal and into the Atlantic Ocean. Going through the famous Panama Canal was very exciting and interesting to Jack.

Miraflores Locks located at the Pacific end of the Panama Canal, February 19, 1948

The Culebra Cut, February 19, 1948 This portion of the canal is where the most excavation was required for the construction of the canal.

In going through the locks, which raised or lowered the ship to a different level, the ship's engines were stopped and the ship was pulled through the locks by two iron mules, little tractors which ran along the lock, one on each side of the ship, and were attached to the ship with cables. Once through the locks, the ship again took off under her own power.

An iron mule at the Pedro Miguel Locks,
February 19, 1948

Another view of the Pedro Miguel Locks and iron mule

On February 25, 1948, the Orion moored to the dock in the Naval Station at Norfolk, Virginia.

While in Norfolk, Jack went home for the weekend. The trip home was a little different than the usual. He left Norfolk on a Navy Transport plane and landed in Washington, D.C. one and a half hours later. He then left Washington by Greyhound bus and arrived at home seven hours later. After the weekend visit, He boarded a Greyhound bus which took him the entire distance from home to Norfolk.

On March 2, 1948, the ship left Norfolk and arrived at the Atlantic entrance to the Panama Canal on March 8th. They went through the canal and moored to the dock at the Rodman Naval Station in Balboa, Canal Zone.

Because Jack liked the fresh air and disliked the togetherness of the ship's sleeping quarters, he always slept on the bridge, sometimes on the open bridge and sometimes in the pilot house. In order not to oversleep and miss breakfast, Jack decided that he needed an alarm clock. He did not have one, so he got one of the ship's boat clocks and unscrewed the glass cover from its face. He then soldered a short piece of stripped wire to the hour hand with the end of the wire extending beyond the edge of the clock. He then hammered a nail into a piece pf wood, with the nail extending above the top of the clock as it laid on its back on the board. He had a small battery operated radio, so he wired around the switch on the radio and attached one wire to the nail and the other to the clock. As the hour hand moved around the clock, it reached a position so that the extended wire from the hour hand made contact with the nail in the board. That completed the circuit and the radio started to play. The nail was located so that the radio would play at the time that Jack wanted to awaken.

For the next three months, the ship did not leave the Rodman Naval base. During that time, Jack went on liberty regularly. On march 10, he went into Panama City, then took the bus to the end of the line in the farming area close to the ruins of old Panama City. When he got off the bus, he walked along a road and came upon the Panama Riding Stables at Parque Lefevre, Panama. There he rented a horse and headed for Old Panama City on horseback. The horse wasn't in any hurry, so, therefore, neither was Jack. Along the way, they came to a gully so the horse walked up to it and stopped. He refused to jump over it. Jack got off the horse, took the reins, and led the horse to the other side of the gully where he remounted the horse and continued his ride to the Old City of Panama. The horse and Jack rode through the ruins of the old city. In 1671, Henry Morgan, the pirate, attacked the city to acquire a golden altar which was in the church. However, the people of Old Panama City knew that the pirate was coming, so before he got there, the golden altar was moved to a church in modern Panama City where it still remains today. Apparently this angered Captain Morgan, so he burned down the entire old City of Panama. The foundations of some buildings still exist, and the church bell tower is still standing, along with a portion of the monastery.

Ruins of Old Panama City, March 28, 1948

Even though the city is destroyed, it has been there a long time and is interesting to walk through and to observe. When Jack rode the horse back to the stables, the horse galloped and, when he came to the gulley, he jumped over it. He was just glad to go back home. Jack went to the ruins of Old Panama City many times, and usually on horseback.

Church tower, Ruins of Old Panama, March 26, 1948

The Llama, June 9, 1948

One time when Jack was in the old ruins, he saw a llama standing in a grassy area among the ruins, so he walked over to talk to the llama and possibly pet him. When he got within several feet of the llama, the llama swung his head around and spit on Jacks white Navy jumper. The results of that was that Jack had a very large blob of brown tobacco juice on the front of his uniform. Jack could have walked over to the ocean, which was nearby, and washed his jumper. It would have dried very quickly because it was a very warm, sunny day. Jack didn't bother to do that. He went back to the ship with his big brown stain on his uniform.

Another interesting place where Jack went, quite a few times, on weekends, was to Taboga Island. Taboga was considered to be a resort island. The transportation to Taboga Island was on a motorboat which ran from the outskirts of Panama City. On the Island, they had cabins that could be rented to spend the night. There was a beach there and a few concession stands. Jack liked to go there because it was different. He enjoyed walking into the jungle on the island, always looking up in the trees to make sure there were no pythons browsing around up there. He would spend the night in a cabin and return to the ship the next day.

One weekend Bob Filkens went along to the island. They sat on the beach, in their swimming trunks for quite a while. While sitting there, a young Panamanian boy offered to climb a pineapple tree and get each of them a nice ripe pineapple.

They each gave him a quarter and gave him the go-ahead. He scaled the tree masterfully and hacked two pineapples loose with his machete, then delivered them to the two of them. Jack ate his pineapple similar to the way in which you would eat a watermelon. He broke the knobby things off of it, then bit into the sweet fruit and ate it in that manner. They each ate their total pineapple, which was juicy and sweet.

Jack eating a pineapple, May 16, 1948

While sitting there, they were observing the ocean and the waves flowing onto the sandy beach. In the distance from where they were sitting, there was a very small island visible. The name of the island was Taboguilla Island. They decided that they would rent a rowboat and go out to that island. So they got the rowboat, still wearing their swimming trunks, and took turns rowing the boat toward the island. Now this was going on very close to the equator, in late

Spring, and it was very warm and sunny. It seemed that they were rowing for hours and the island was not getting any closer. They did consider on several occasions to give it up and go back to Taboga Island, but they gave that idea up and continued to row toward the island.

Jack rowing to Taboguilla Island, May 16, 1948

Eventually, they did arrive at the island. It was probably about one hundred feet in diameter, contained about two or three trees, and a few big rocks, plus the ruins of a cabin that someone had built many years before.

The cabin on Taboguilla Island, May, 16, 1948.

Filkins contemplating the journey, back to Taboga Island, May 16, 1948

They dragged their rowboat about 20 feet onto the land, then went swimming in the beautiful, extremely clear, water. After about an hour or two, they decided to start back toward Taboga Island. They walked over to get their boat and it was about fifty feet from the edge of the water. The tide had gone out and left the boat higher from the water. With that, Jack, who was the Quartermaster and was the expert on such things, remembered that the tide in the area around Panama actually has a differential level of about 20 vertical feet from low tide to high tide. They realized then, had the tide come in instead of out, their boat would have floated away leaving them stranded on their little island. With that cheerful thought in their heads, they got back into the boat and took turns rowing, and finally reached the shore at Taboga Island.

At the end of the weekend, they went back to their ship. The next morning, they woke up and realized that they were badly sunburned all over their bodies, they had sand flea bites from sitting on the sandy beach, and their lips were sore from being exposed to the pineapple acid. Uncomfortable? No, that word was not harsh enough.

Filkens was an electrician's mate, so he worked in a different area of the ship than Jack did. They did not see each other while they recuperated. The ship did not go out to sea for several weeks after the great boat ride. Jack handled the situation by staying on the bridge, away from most of the crew. And to avoid having his uniform rubbing his sore sunburn, the only clothing that Jack wore for several weeks was his underpants. It seemed forever, but finally the pain stopped and they both got back to normal.

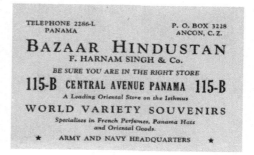

Jack drinking coconut milk from a coconut
with a straw, June 9, 1948, Panama

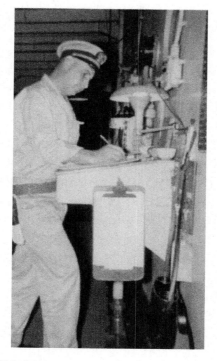

Chief Warrant Boatswain McCarty
Officer of the Deck August 23, 1948

Most of the Officers of the Deck were pleasant people, therefore, while on watch there would be conversation. Bos'un McCarty was a very happy and pleasant person, so when Jack was on watch with him, there would be much conversation. This one time Jack told McCarty that the next day, when he goes on liberty, he is going to go down to the swamps, located nearby, to get a look at some alligators. McCarty's response was, "Can you run 21 miles per hour?" Surprised, Jack answered that he could not. McCarty said, " Alligators can run 20 miles per hour." Jack did not go to the swamps to see the alligators.

While on the Orion, in the evening, when in port, Jack would go to the Chart House where it was quiet. There he would read, or write letters, or sometimes visit with others. In the charthouse, hanging on the bulkhead, was a very large radio measuring about three feet square and fifteen inches deep. He used to listen to music on that radio most of the time that he was in the chart house. The station that he preferred was a Panamanian station that played good lively Latin music. There was also an American Armed Forces Radio Station that played American music which he occasionally listened to. However, Jack preferred the Panamanian music to the modern American music. The only way to listen to the music on that radio was to plug in, and wear, earphones. The radio had no speaker. Jack got tired of the confinement of sitting in one place wearing the earphones, so he looked for a solution. In the charthouse there was a fathometer, an instrument used for measuring the depth of the ocean. The fathometer had a speaker in it to allow the operator to listen to the initial ping signal to the bottom of the ocean, then an echo ping. First Jack tried to find some terminals on the radio to which he could connect the speaker. He was reaching into the narrow space behind the radio trying to find something when he apparently found some live electrical terminals. When he touched them he got jolted and went flying across the chart house. Concluding that this search was not a good idea, he thought of another way to solve the problem. He cut the wires loose from the headphones and attached an extension wire to the end of the wires where the headphone had been. He ran the wires along the bulkhead, in a way that was not too obvious, and connected them into the terminals of the speaker in the fathometer. Using the original earphone plug, he plugged the wiring in to the radio in the same manner as he had been plugging in the earphones. He was successful. Music came out of the fathometer speaker. For his remaining time on the ship, he listened to music coming from the fathometer speaker. When Jack was transferred off the ship, he left the radio connected to the fathometer. He liked to think that someday a navigator would turn on the fathometer and the popular song entitled, "How deep is the ocean" would flow from the speaker.

While serving on board the Orion at the Balboa Naval Station in the Panama Canal Zone, the ship cruised out into the Pacific Ocean just for routine training. The Orion served as a target for the submarines. The submarines would fire their unloaded torpedos at the Orion, but low enough in the water that they would not hit the bottom of the Orion, but would pass beneath the keel.

Jack steering the USS Orion
In a rather casual way
May 15, 1948

While on that cruise, the ship anchored at an uninhabited island called San Jose Island. The island had a large, sandy beach. The ship sent boats to shore with anyone who would like to go to the beach. The sailors wore their swimming trunks on the boat, so they were properly attired when they reached the beach, however, when they got close to the shore, the boats stopped and their operators said that was as far as they could go and told the crew of the ship to swim ashore. Not realizing that the boat was about 300 feet from the shore, everyone jumped into the water and started swimming for shore, including Jack. Jack was in good physical condition, but his swimming ability was not too good. He was capable of swimming about fifty feet at the time. So he kept swimming doggie paddle long after he couldn't swim any more. He had to. Other swimmers came alongside him and encouraged him to keep swimming. Finally, Jack reached the shore, but was totally fatigued. He crawled onto the beach, as did many of the others, and laid there to rest. Upon getting back into shape, they enjoyed the beach for several hours then it was time to go back to the ship. For the return trip, the boat came much closer to the shore and everyone, including Jack, comfortably swam back to the boat and rode back to the ship.

Jack on San Jose Island. This photo was taken with Jack's camera which he took ashore in an inflated aerological balloon. June 16, 1948

The next day, they did the same thing, except this time the boats went in closer to the shore. Jack was the only person to take a camera ashore. He put his camera inside a large aerological balloon, added a little air, and tied it shut. Swimming into shore, he pushed the balloon ahead of him in the water. On shore, he took the camera out of the balloon and took pictures. When they left the beach, he put the camera back into the balloon and pushed it back to the waiting boat, which took them back to the ship. The next day, the Orion returned to the Rodman Naval base.

The Orion spent much of her time tied to the dock at the Rodman naval Base. While in port, the Quartermasters stood their watch on the quarterdeck with the Officer of the Deck. Many of these four hour watches dragged on because there was nothing happening. Jack found a way to amuse himself, and others. In the small office on the quarterdeck, they had a small, bound book which was called the morning call book. The purpose of the book was for people to enter their name and bunk location and the time that they wanted to be awakened so that the messenger of the watch could come to their bunk at the right time and awaken them. These names were entered at the front of the book and continued through the book as time passed. Jack started at the back of the book and worked forward with his entries.

Jack drew pictures of his imaginary monsters on the pages of the book. Each time he was on watch, he would add some new ones. The other people who had to stand their watch at the same location, including the officers of the deck, would arrive at their post at the proper time. The first thing that each of them would do was to open the book to the back pages to look at the new pictures. The following is an example of that great artwork that entertained so many.

WILL McSHERRY CATCH THE RABBIT BEFORE THE BEAR CATCHES McSHERRY?

A young man, named Tremblay was a crew member of the Orion. Even though he was probably only about 18 years old, he had a pilot's license. On August 30, Jack & Tremblay rented a Cessna 120 at the Paitilla airport and flew over Panama City for twenty minutes.

The next day, Filkins and Jack played golf on the Naval Ammunition Depot golf course. Jack never played golf before on a real golf course. They only played 9 holes and had large enough scores to qualify for 18 holes, so they called it a day. They had a little incident on the golf course that day. While teeing off at one of the holes, Jack was preparing to hit the ball toward the next hole when two marines walked across the area in front of them. Jack was on top of a hill and the next hole was on high ground behind the two marines, so he whacked the ball as hard as he could assuming that the ball would fly over their heads and toward the next hole. That was exactly what happened. However, the marines were not impressed. They stood there and screamed at Jack for not yelling "fore". Jack figured if they were dumb enough to walk in front of him when he was preparing to hit the ball, it didn't hurt them to listen to the whizzing of the ball as it flew over their heads.

Jack playing golf, Sept. 1, 1948

On September 5, 1948, Jack and Tremblay decided to rent a plane and fly to Costa Rica to go swimming on the beach. So they went to the local airport and rented a plane. It was a two seater. Jack sat alongside the pilot. The pilot was Tremblay.

They took off and were heading for Costa Rica when a big black cloud appeared ahead of them. It filled about half of the sky. Tremblay said they better return to Panama. In all of his wisdom, Jack suggested that they could turn eastward and fly around the black clouds. He had no clue to what he was talking about. But Tremblay said that he supposed they could do that, and they did. They managed to go around the storm and were finally approaching their destination. Tremblay looked at his chart and told Jack that he could not find the airport where they were supposed to land. Finally, he decided that the grass area below, with some car tracks on it, must be the airport. He was making an approach to land, but when they were about fifty feet above the ground, a cow walked out in front of them. Tremblay gunned the engine and went up higher. Even though the cow walked out in front of them, Tremblay was still sure that they were at the airport, so he circled around and made a landing in the grassy area. It was the airport.

They left the plane and walked to the beach. It was a nice day and they enjoyed the water. After several hours, they headed back to the plane. Along the way, they watched some spider monkeys playing. They boarded the plane and flew back to Panama.

Jack holding a spider monkey at Santa Clara
Beach. September 5, 1948

Tremblay, Sept. 5, 1948 Santa Clara Beach, Costa Rica

Cessna 140, Santa Clara
September 5, 1948

On the 7th of September, and again on the 10th of September, Tremblay and Jack again played golf on the naval Ammunition Depot golf course

N A D
Golf Course

Balboa
Canal Zone

RULES

1. **Out of Bounds**
   A. All fences and macadem roads loss of distance only.
   B. Fence to the left of No. 2 fairway. Loss of stroke and distance.
2. **Hazards**
   Ball may be removed with no penalty from tile ditch running axially from hole No. 4, ditch between culvert and bridge on No. 5 tee shot, and tile ditch in front of No. 7 green on tee shot. All other tile diches ball may be taken out and placed no nearer green --- Penalty one stroke.
3. **Lost and Unplayable Ball**
   If a ball is lost or be deemed by the player to be unplayable the player shall play his next stroke as nearly as possible at the spot from which the ball is lost, or is unplayable --- Penalty, one stroke. At man - made hazards, ball may be removed three card lengths without penalty.
4. **Winter Rules Apply ---**
   ### ETIQUETTE OF GOLF
1. **Order of Precedence**
   A. Twosome; Threesome; Foursome.
   B. Players following shall be allowed to play through when ball is apparently lost.
   C. Do not play into preceding players without their permission.
2. **Replace All Turf and Divots**
3. **Read the Rules of Golf posted in 19th hole!**

Date _7 SEPT. 1948_

OUT

MCSHERRY / TRIMBLAY / PAVLIK

Hole	Yds	Mens Par	Ladies Par	Hdcp						
1	146	3	3	8	3	8	9			
2	254	4	4	4	9	12	7			
3	296	4	5	1	15	12	9			
4	222	3	4	6	5	7	5			
5	308	4	4	3	9	9	6			
6	284	4	5	2	9	9	8			
7	284	3	4	5	9	10	10			
8	206	3	3	7	9	5	7			
9	130	3	3	9	12	9	8			
Out	2130	31	35		80	81	69			

Scored By: _J. H. Medbery jr._

IN

Hole	Yds	Mens Par	Ladies Par	Hdcp						
10	146	3	3	8						
11	254	4	4	4						
12	296	4	5	1						
13	222	3	4	6						
14	308	4	4	3						
15	284	4	5	2						
16	284	3	4	5						
17	206	3	3	7						
18	130	3	3	9						
In	2130	31	35							
Out	2130	31	35							
Total	4260	62	70							
Hdcp										
Net										

Attested By: _____

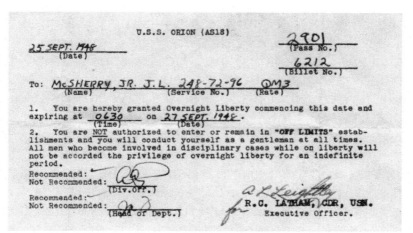

```
                    U.S.S. ORION (AS18)
                                                2901
25 SEPT. 1948                                  (Pass No.)
    (Date)
                                                6212
                                               (Billet No.)

To: McSHERRY, JR. J.L. 248-72-96   QM3
       (Name)              (Service No.)    (Rate)

1.    You are hereby granted Overnight Liberty commencing this date and
expiring at   0630    on  27 SEPT. 1948 .
            (Time)         (Date)
2.    You are NOT authorized to enter or remain in "OFF LIMITS" estab-
lishments and you will conduct yourself as a gentleman at all times.
All men who become involved in disciplinary cases while on liberty will
not be accorded the privilege of overnight liberty for an indefinite
period.
Recommended:
Not Recommended:
               (Div.Off.)
Recommended:
Not Recommended:                        R.C. LATHAM, CDR, USN.
               (Head of Dept.)             Executive Officer.
```

Emilia Garcia, Taboga Island, Sept. 26, 1948

While on the Orion, as Jack's enlistment was nearing its termination, he decided to begin practicing to be a civilian. To do this, he had to speak in civilian terminology rather than in nautical terminology. He got most of his practice while standing quartermaster watch on the quarterdeck. One of the quartermaster's duties while on watch was to go to the bridge every hour to read and record the temperature, the barometric pressure, the humidity and the wind velocity. To leave the quarterdeck, it was required that he would have to salute the officer of the deck and request permission to go to the bridge to read the instruments. Of course, permission was always granted. With his civilian terminology, Jack thereafter approached the officer of the deck saluted him, and requested permission to go upstairs to get the weather readings for recording in the ship's log. Or, if he wanted to leave the quarterdeck to go to the living quarters to wake up his relief, he would ask permission to go to the bedroom to wake up his relief. The deck was called the floor. The bulkheads were referred to as the wall, and the overhead was referred to as the ceiling. Instead of going forward on the deck, he would go up front. By this procedure he was able to revert back to civilian status, some of the officers accepted this with a smile, others merely snarled.

THE PANAMA CANAL
CASH SALE RECEIPT

N°. 899907

Name _Mr. J. L. McSherryJ._ Identification Card _____ Date _10/13/4___, 19__

MR 55465—Panama Canal—1-5-47—1,000 books

ACCOUNT NO.	QUANTITY	DESCRIPTION	UNIT	PRICE	AMOUNT
	1	ea Am Nautical Almanac 1949	1	ea	1 50

Original—To purchaser
Duplicate—To Comptroller, The Panama Canal
Triplicate—To Store Section for disposition
Quadruplicate—To remain in book

RECEIVED PAYMENT

T. A. Loucker
Cashier

Amount_ 1 50
Plus ___ %_
TOTAL_ 1 50

On October 14, the Orion got underway from Balboa enroute to New London, Connecticut. After a week in New London, the ship got underway, and two days later anchored in Lynhaven Roads, Virginia. While there, they participated in operations at sea with other ships of the fleet.

While cruising in formation with other ships of the fleet at a speed of 15 knots, the ships were commanded by the flagship to increase speed to flank speed. Flank speed is the top speed that the ship can logically do. The Orion had to radio back that they were doing flank speed. They were doing sixteen knots and that is all they could do. Jack was embarrassed, being a cruiser sailor, he was used to flank speed being about thirty three knots. So the fleet moved ahead at flank speed and the Orion kept lagging further behind as time passed.

Four days later, the Orion moored to the dock in Norfolk, Virginia. While in Norfolk, Jack went to a concert by Paul Whiteman and his orchestra at the Norfolk Auditorium. The concert featured the music of George Gershwin. The music as played by the Paul Whiteman orchestra was beautiful and very impressive.

On November 15, the Orion got underway from Norfolk and moored to the dock in Coco Solo, Canal Zone, on November 20. The next day they left Coco Solo and went through the Panama Canal and moored to the dock in Balboa.

Christmas display at the United States Army Base in the Panama Canal Zone. December 25, 1948, Santa's sled was a tank, and the reindeer were jeeps.

Baldy, USS Orion
December 27, 1948

Jack having bananas for lunch,
January 22, 1949

Lassalle, also having bananas for lunch, but not as many.
Balboa, Canal Zone, January 22, 1949

While the Orion was tied to the dock at Rodman Naval Base in Balboa, Canal Zone, Jack and Lassalle were on the signal bridge passing the time of day when a destroyer flying the Chinese flag entered the harbor and was heading toward the docks.

They decided to try to make contact with the signalmen on the destroyer. They flashed the signal light toward the destroyer with the international code letters to make contact. The Chinese signalman responded. Through the signaling, they learned that his name was Yeh Kwang-Lung. Jack & Lassalle invited him to come to the Orion for a visit, which he did. They had a good visit. Yeh Kwang-Lung was a very polite and interesting person. He spoke some English. Neither Lassalle or Jack could speak Chinese.

Yeh Kwang-Lung then invited Jack and Lassalle to come to his ship to visit. They did just that. The Chinese destroyer was formerly an American destroyer which was given to the Chinese Government by the united States Government. It was interesting to walk around on the ship which was totally occupied by Chinese sailors.

Jack & Yeh Kwang-Lung on board the Chinese destroyer
RCS Tai Tsang. Jan. 22, 1949.

Jack and Lassalle on board the Chinese Destroyer RCS Tai Tsang. Balboa, Canal Zone, January 22, 1949.

U. S. S. ORION

From: Dental Officer.

To   :   _6_ Division Officer.

The below named man has a dental appointment for _0930_ on _1-25-49_ 19_____.

Name _McSherry, J. L._ Rate _2m3_

It is requested that he be instructed to appear at the above time.

J. H. Mathis DSI

Lassalle, a Brazilian Sailor, and Filkins on the Brazilian ship,
Almirante Saldanha, Feb. 3, 1949. Balboa, Canal Zone.

On February 7, 1949, Jack was transferred from the USS Orion to the USS President Jackson for transportation to Norfolk, Virginia where he would be discharged from the Navy upon the completion of his enlistment in the Navy. The President Jackson anchored at Guantanamo Bay, Cuba, for one day along the route to Norfolk. On February 15, The President Jackson docked in Norfolk, where Jack was transferred to the Separation Center, Naval Air Station, Norfolk , Virginia to await his discharge from the Navy.

While waiting for his discharge date, Jack went home on liberty for a weekend.

On March 9, 1949, Jack was honorably discharged from the Navy, having served three years, eleven months, and twenty three days. He was discharged four days before his enlistment expired.

When Jack was discharged from the Navy, he was awarded the following medals:

American Campaign Medal, 1941-1946

Victory Medal, World War II

Occupation Medal, World War II, 1945-1957

And, Yes, The Navy Good Conduct Medal

He was discharged with the rank of Quartermaster third class, and wore one hash mark representing four years of service.

When Jack enlisted in the Navy, he weighed 129 pounds. At the time of his discharge, four years later, he weighed 165 pounds and it was all muscle, no fat.

Jack is now a civilian and has grown into manhood.

One of the first things Jack did when he got home was to take a carload of his friends to attend a concert by Spike Jones and his City Slickers at Lakewood Park, located near Mahanoy City, Pennsylvania.

Spike Jones was a musical genius and his band consisted of the perfection in musicians.

DICK MORGAN

FREDDY MORGAN

BIA SOUEZ

PAUL JUDSON

DICK GARDNER

MUSICAL MADNESS

Introducing to you photographically,
the Stars of Spike Jones'
hilarious Musical Depreciation Review,
featuring the renowned City Slickers.

DR. HORATIO Q. BIRDBATH

BILL KING

SIR FREDRIC GAS

FRANK LITTLE

BETTYJO HUSTON

HELEN GRAYCO

DOODLES WEAVER

GEORGE ROCK

THE SLICKERETTES

CHAPTER VII

JACK REACHED MANHOOD

Now at the age of 21, and having served four years in the Navy, and having survived the slings and arrows of that service, Jack has earned the right to be classed as a man.

What is the definition of manhood? Manhood can be based on many factors.

A man accepts his responsibilities.

He is honest, and totally trustworthy in all of his activities.

A man thinks for himself and does not follow the goading and prompting by others.

He judges other people only on the basis of their dependability, goodness and kindness. There is no room in manhood for those who look down on other people, and discriminate against them, because of national origin, skin color, religion, or other personal features.

A man does not claim to be superior to others.

A man is kind, friendly, cheerful, helpful, and generous toward others.

A man is polite and kind to ladies, children and strangers.

A man is kind to all living creatures on this earth.

When a man makes a promise, he keeps that promise.

Some factors that are not necessary for manhood, and, in fact, are detrimental to manhood, are as follows:

Excessive use of alcoholic beverages.

Smoking of cigarettes.

Use of recreational, mind-numbing drugs.

Use of foul language.

Cruelty to children and animals

An obstinate or arrogant attitude.

This book was written from the memory of Jack L. McSherry, Jr., who typed it into the computer. The computer was quite often contrary which created many arguments between Jack and the computer. Jack has no computer abilities and quite often pushes the wrong buttons. Fortunately, Jack's granddaughter, Christina McSherry is a computer genius and always came to his assistance whenever necessary. Thank you Christina. This book could not have been created without your calm and expert assistance.

Goodbye, thanks for reading, and have a good day.

Jack L. McSherry, Jr.

Printed in Great Britain
by Amazon

28172979R00106